The Cops & Robbers Holiday Club

Barnabas for Children® is a registered word mark and the logo is a registered device mark of The Bible Reading Fellowship.

Published by
The Bible Reading Fellowship
15 The Chambers, Vineyard
Abingdon OX14 3FE
United Kingdom
Tel: +44 (0)1865 319700
Email: enquiries@brf.org.uk
Website: www.brf.org.uk
BRF is a Registered Charity

ISBN 978 0 85746 111 7

First published 2014
10 9 8 7 6 5 4 3 2 1 0

Acknowledgments
Unless otherwise stated, scripture quotations are taken from the Contemporary English Version of the Bible published by HarperCollins Publishers, copyright © 1991, 1992, 1995 American Bible Society.

Scripture quotations taken from the Holy Bible, New International Version (Anglicised edition), copyright © 1979, 1984, 2011 by Biblica (formerly International Bible Society), are used by permission of Hodder & Stoughton Publishers, an Hachette UK company. All rights reserved. 'NIV' is a registered trademark of Biblica (formerly International Bible Society). UK trademark number 1448790.

A catalogue record for this book is available from the British Library

Printed by Gutenberg Press, Tarxien, Malta

The Cops & Robbers Holiday Club

A five-day holiday club plan, complete and ready to run

John Hardwick

Acknowledgments

With thanks to the following people for their help and inspiration:

Steve Whyatt, with whom I share a small office and who has to put up with me writing and practising the songs and sketches day after day.

My wife Rachel and children Chloe and Ben.

Sue Doggett and Olivia Warburton, my ever-patient editors.

David Wilkinson, for the sheet music notation on pages 18–20 and 22–27.

St John's Parish Church, Woodbridge, for allowing me to try out my new theme on you and for coming up with ideas.

St Columba Church, Portadown, for piloting *Cops & Robbers*.

Contents

Appendices

Important information

Photocopy permission

The right to photocopy material in *The Cops & Robbers Holiday Club* is granted for the pages that contain the photocopying clause, 'Reproduced with permission from *The Cops & Robbers Holiday Club* by John Hardwick, published by Barnabas for Children 2014: www.barnabasinchurches.org.uk', so long as reproduction is for use in a teaching situation by the original purchaser. The right to photocopy material is not granted for anyone other than the original purchaser without written permission from BRF.

The Copyright Licensing Agency (CLA)

If you are resident in the UK and you have a photocopying licence with the Copyright Licensing Agency (CLA), please check the terms of your licence. If your photocopying request falls within the terms of your licence, you may proceed without seeking further permission. If your request exceeds the terms of your CLA licence, please contact the CLA direct with your request. Copyright Licensing Agency, Saffron House, 6–10 Kirby Street, London EC1N 8TS. Telephone 020 7400 3100; fax 020 7400 3101; email cla@cla.co.uk; website www.cla.co.uk. The CLA will provide photocopying authorisation and royalty fee information on behalf of BRF.

BRF is a Registered Charity (No. 233280)

Foreword

With his experience and passion for reaching children with the life-changing story of the gospel, John Hardwick in my view is a tough act to follow. His enthusiasm will have you joining in, no matter what your age. Somehow, John will have you standing, moving joints you didn't know you had... he reminds me of a jelly on a plate, always moving and colourful! Children love the vibrancy and freedom they find through his music and books and the simplicity of his work.

Through the pages of *The Cops & Robbers Holiday Club*, John sets out a map that will bring children, in particular, to know what it is to be free and to forgive. Having had the experience of prison and being set free,

I feel that the reality has been captured perfectly within this resource.

'I love change and am passionate about the freedom found in Christ. I am excited about doing the impossible.' Seldom do you find such talent as John has and uses so well for the God he loves, bringing freedom, fun and sincerity. I have no hesitation in recommending *The Cops & Robbers Holiday Club* to any church with a heart for reaching younger generations through drama, music, craft activities and games.

Clive Cornish

Introduction

'Hello, hello, hello—what's going on here?' Years ago, my father was leading a beach mission (a bit like a holiday club, but on a beach), and our theme that day was 'Jesus is alive'. A man who had had a little too much to drink declared at the top of his voice, 'No, Jesus isn't alive, he's dead!'

'He's very much alive,' my father replied.

'Prove it,' said the man.

A lively discussion followed and I could see everyone on the beach beginning to sit up and listen. Suddenly a policeman appeared and the man who had had a little too much to drink said, 'If you want to know the answer, ask a policeman! Excuse me, Mr Policeman, can you please tell me, Officer, is Jesus dead or alive?' Without any hesitation the policeman said in a loud and confident voice, 'I am 100 per cent convinced that Jesus is alive!' Everyone looked amazed as the policeman went on to say how the police have to piece together all the evidence to find out the truth when it comes to solving crimes, and he had applied the same principle when it came to the life of Jesus—concluding that Jesus is alive. We cheered!

'Cops and Robbers' is a great theme for so many reasons. From the early days of silent films and *Keystone Cops*, through classics such as *Dixon of Dock Green*, *Z Cars*, *Softly, Softly* and *Starsky and Hutch*, to more recent crime series such as *CSI* and *Cops on Camera*, police dramas have always been firm favourites with TV audiences. They are exciting, fast-paced, high-action adventures with a mystery to solve, grabbing people's imaginations. One of the key messages is usually (although not always) the theme of good overcoming bad, often accompanied by sound advice to encourage the viewers to take care and do the right thing.

The theme of 'Cops and Robbers' remains hugely popular. People of all ages love to see how good eventually prevails—although this is not always the case. The story invariably includes a plot in which a crime is committed. The consequences are then played out, with innocent parties sometimes being falsely accused and perhaps even punished for an offence they didn't commit. The adventure then takes us through the process of exoneration and, finally, forgiveness as good wins through.

The Bible contains many stories of people who enabled good to triumph because of their belief and trust in God. There were also 'Bible baddies' who disobeyed God and turned his people away from him. Sometimes, however, the Bible baddies changed and became goodies. *The Cops & Robbers Holiday Club* is based on the life of Joseph and explores the many lessons we can learn through his amazing story. The story of Joseph is one of the best-known in the Bible, and many children will be familiar with Andrew Lloyd Webber's popular musical *Joseph and the Amazing Technicolor Dreamcoat*.

Out of Jacob's twelve sons, Joseph was his favourite, which caused big problems among his siblings. Jealous of the attention their father lavished on him, Joseph's brothers came up with a plot, which led them to commit a terrible crime. Joseph was taken away, and later, just as he was maturing into a good guy, he was falsely accused and sent to jail. However, because Joseph continually believed and trusted in God, this once-spoilt child was eventually exonerated and granted his freedom, which he used to save others. Put in a position of trust and power, he then faced an inner battle and hard choices as he struggled to forgive his brothers and, after many years of being apart, reunite the family.

These themes also tie in with the life of Jesus. Those who were jealous of Jesus plotted against him, which led to a most terrible crime being committed. Jesus, the innocent party, was falsely accused and condemned to die on the cross. But, in a twist to the tale, it is we who are exonerated when Jesus wins the ultimate battle between good and evil. He died for our freedom and, when we put our belief and trust in him, he forgives us and welcomes us into his wonderful family.

The theme also raises the issue of children who, like Joseph, come from homes full of hurt and misunderstanding. Even when lives are messed up, good can prevail. God's constant love for Joseph and his family brought good out of bad, and his constant love can enable good to win through in our lives, too.

Setting up for a holiday club

To set the scene for your holiday club, you could select police ranks such as Constable, Sergeant, Inspector, Chief Inspector, Superintendent and Chief Superintendent for member names and appropriate dress for your leaders and assistants. You'll need craft leaders to lead crafts and games, a (police fitness training camp) manager to oversee the sessions, and floating helpers to assist with the general running of the sessions. Choose team colours and names to match the theme.

Decorate your venue in keeping with the theme. The walls of the room could include posters of police TV programmes and film police. Include title words and slogans like 'The Plot', 'The Crime', 'Evidence', 'Police Station' and 'Go to Jail'. You could also include pictures of police cars, English police, American cops and old-fashioned prisoners with shackles on their ankles. There are hundreds of images you can find on the internet (but do be aware that copyright restrictions may apply to some). Maybe you could have a blue flashing light, with sirens playing quietly in the background. There is plenty of scope for dressing up as 'cops and robbers'.

Because the Bible stories are based on the life of Joseph, you could include an Egyptian theme too.

Holiday club roles and responsibilities

Good team work is essential for good children's work. As well as an overall holiday club coordinator, you'll need people to fill all the following roles. Depending on the size of your club, these roles need to be allocated to one person per role, or doubled up as appropriate. For example, the registration officer could also be responsible for the refreshments, or the person responsible for publicity could also act as a floater.

Registration officer

This role would suit a well-organised person. If the children are registered before the start date of the holiday club, you will save time on the first day of the club. If you choose to register the children on the first day, you will need a good team of helpers to cope with the workload.

You need to register the following details for each child:

- Child's name
- Address
- Date of birth
- Contact phone number
- Medical details (such as asthma or allergies)
- Parent's or guardian's permission for child to attend the club

You will need to split children into groups according to their age bands, and possibly subsection them into teams. It's advisable to issue each child with a colour-coded sticker or badge to identify him or her and the team to which they belong. Have a 'welcome' team available 15 minutes before the start to make the children feel at home when they arrive.

Team leaders

Team leaders need to be able to deal with a high level of responsibility. Each team leader will be allocated to a particular group of children or age band. They will stay with the children the whole time, sitting with them and leading them through various activities. They will befriend, enthuse and maintain a level of control. It's important that team leaders join in the songs, as children will look to them as role models.

Team helpers

These are people who can help the team leader. They need to be free to fetch things, accompany children to the toilet and so on.

Games leader

This needs to be someone with experience of sorting children quickly, and accustomed to organising games. A powerful voice would be an asset. Keep the games in one location and bring the children to that area when it is their turn to play.

Craft leader

This needs to be someone able to organise a simple craft activity. The craft leader will need to start collecting materials well in advance. Try to make the crafts theme-related. Once again, have a fixed location for crafts and bring the children to that area when it is their turn.

Time keeper

This person watches the time and gives a five-minute warning to activity leaders that the session is about to end. He or she then rings a bell when it's time for the teams to move on to the next activity.

Snack team

One person or team is needed to prepare drinks and biscuits for the children. Not all the children will need their drinks at the same time, as teams will take turns to have their refreshments. Please ensure that all the leaders, including the games leader and craft leader, also receive drinks.

First aider

It is essential to have someone available who is a trained first aider, and to have a well-stocked first aid box. St John Ambulance may be able to offer advice if you are unsure about how to provide this facility.

Discipler

Children may have questions about the Christian faith. Disciplers need to be able to talk in simple language and be good listeners. They should know what they believe and how to put it across without manipulation or forcing the children into making statements or promises they cannot understand or keep.

You will need to think about how to follow up children who are seeking to know more about the Christian faith.

Publicity officer

This person is needed to design and organise posters, leaflets and school visits, and to contact the local press.

Floaters

Floaters are helpers who cannot commit themselves to the whole week's programme but are able to come for a day or two. They can help wherever there is a need.

Stage team or presenter

Either one person or a team is needed to lead the up-front programme, leading the songs, theme illustration, quiz, Bible story and teaching, and introducing the drama and puppet sketches. You may wish to fill this role from your own team, or you may decide to give your regular children's leaders a rest and bring in someone from outside.

Dos and don'ts

Whether you are running a holiday club or weekly midweek sessions, best practice for children's work relies on good teamwork.

- Do create structure and routine so that everyone knows what to expect.
- Do sit in with the children during up-front time.
- Do be prepared to join in songs and interactive parts of the programme. Don't forget that children will look to the team leaders as their role models.
- Do encourage, befriend and control your team of children.
- Do use your common sense.
- Do encourage children to go to the toilet during the activities times rather than the up-front/teaching times. Remember that children follow each other's lead: if you're not careful, all the young ones will decide at once that they need an outing to the toilet.
- Do expect to have fun yourself and be open to learn. The teaching aspect of the programme is not just for the kids. God may choose to speak to you, too.
- Don't loiter on the edge, chatting or distracting the children or presenter as the programme is taking place.
- Don't try to talk over children (or leaders and helpers, for that matter); expect everyone to listen.
- Don't allow leaders and helpers to make up their own rules. Everyone needs to agree what is acceptable behaviour and what isn't.
- Don't allow leaders to sit on the sidelines. They need to join in, too.

Safety first

To safeguard children and to maintain the well-being of the children and members of the team, child protection guidelines should be observed at all times. Any questions relating to Disclosure and Barring Service (DBS) checks should be raised with your church council, diocese or denominational body well before your holiday club start date. The points below are for general guidance only and are not intended to replace official documents concerning the Safeguarding Vulnerable Groups Act 2006, such as Every Child Matters (DfES) and Safe from Harm (Home Office 1993).

- No team member should be alone with a child where their activity cannot be seen by others.
- Always treat the children with respect and dignity.
- Never use physical punishment.
- Ensure that more than one person is present if a child needs to be washed or helped in the toilet.
- Male team members should not accompany female children to the toilet.
- Do not become overfriendly, with children sitting on your lap, hugging or rough-and-tumbling.
- Do not play-fight with children or join in games where you could fall on a child.
- Do not run around with children on your shoulders.
- Do not go into a room alone with a child and never arrange to meet a child alone.
- Avoid any inappropriate touching or any excessively rough or physical games.
- Do not engage in any scapegoating, ridiculing or rejection of a child.
- Do not invite a child to your home alone.
- Avoid giving lifts to children on their own. If a car journey is necessary, a second person should be present and the child should sit on a rear seat of the car, using an appropriate seat belt.
- If you need to contact a child at home during or after the holiday club, ensure that you identify yourself as a member of the holiday club team.
- If abuse is suspected, do not encourage the child to talk further. Report suspicions immediately to the holiday club coordinator and make written notes of anything you and the child said to each other.
- Have someone on security to stop children from wandering out or strangers from wandering into your premises.

Fire safety

- Do not use candles, matches or lighters on the premises.
- Familiarise yourself with the fire exits.
- Observe fire drills: they are for everybody's safety.

Stay legal

Depending on the length of your holiday club session and for how many days it runs, you may need to register with OFSTED.

For up-to-date information about legal requirements for childcare and child protection, contact your local council, your diocese or church office, or:

OFSTED
www.ofsted.gov.uk
www.ofsted.gov.uk/Ofsted-home/Forms-and-guidance

Disclosure and Barring Service
DBS Customer Services
PO Box 110, Liverpool L69 3JD
Tel: 0870 9090811
Email: customerservices@dbs.gsi.gov.uk
Website: www.gov.uk/government/organisations/disclosure-and-barring-service

The Churches Child Protection Advisory Service
PO Box 133, Swanley, Kent BR8 7UQ
Telephone: 0845 120 4550
Fax: 0845 120 4552
Email: info@ccpas.co.uk
Website: www.ccpas.co.uk

Incentives

Throughout our lives we have incentives to help us achieve our very best, and to keep up our enthusiasm and excitement for the job in hand. In schools, children are awarded stars or house points and receive qualifications, which reflect their achievements. In the workplace, there are company perks and the opportunity of promotion or a pay rise. Incentives can help with the boredom of routine. There is always a new target to reach.

With a personal achievement chart or a team achievement score board, children can earn points that are visible on a card, scoring chart or token. They earn points for:

- Attendance
- Answering a question in the quiz

- Being the coolest-behaved girl or boy
- Being outstanding at joining in activities
- Bringing along a friend

Each leader can be given a certain number of tokens to give out at each session. For example, during the Bible story, look out for a couple of children who are really paying attention; during the songs, look out for those joining in well, and so on. The tokens should be given out sparingly to those who deserve them. Most of the children will earn a token, one way or another.

This will help to create an enjoyable holiday club where the children are keen to come, session after session or week after week, and join in all the activities. Do your best to make sure that the up-front teaching time is as enjoyable as any other part of the session.

Action words

Action words are used to grab children's attention instantly as follows:

- Straight: Children sit up with arms folded, ready to listen.
- Serious: Children sit up with arms folded, looking serious.
- Cool: Children brush their hair back with their fingers, looking cool.

Always finish the action words by saying 'Straight' to get the children ready to listen to the Bible story, puppet sketch and so on. You may choose to give a prize token to the child who is the first to sit up straight, ready to listen.

Timetable

A two-and-a-half hour programme (adaptable to suit your situation)	
30 minutes beforehand	Team meet together to pray
15 minutes beforehand	Last-minute preparation
00.00	Open doors for registration. Split the children into three teams, according to their ages. Children go to team leaders, who are waiting in the team areas.
00.15	Up-front presentation 1: • Welcome and action words (see page 14 for action words) • Opening talk • Theme song plus other song (see pages 18, 22–27 for details) • Puppet sketch • Theme illustration • Memory verse • The Watt family daily drama • Song or memory verse recap
00.45	Activity time: three activities, each lasting for 25 minutes. In their teams, the children rotate round the different activities so that all the children do each activity: • Game • Craft • Snack, chat and fun sheet, plus optional prayer activity in small groups
02.00	Up-front presentation 2: • Song (as children return) and memory verse recap • Quick quiz • Song (if time) • Bible story and message • Round-up and final prayer • Theme song
02.30	Children go back to small groups and wait to be collected. NB: It is important to work out a routine for collection, so that children cannot leave the premises without an accompanying parent or guardian.

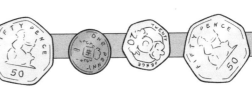

Teaching outlines

Day 1: The plot

Don't be jealous!

- Opening talk: Jealousy often causes crime.
- Puppet sketch: Lucy is cross with her little brother because he has lent his Beano to someone else.
- Bible memory verse: 'I know the plans I have for you,' declares the Lord, 'plans to prosper you and not to harm you, plans to give you hope and a future.' (Jeremiah 29:11, NIV)
- The Watt family: Some robbers steal Grandma Watt's strawberry cream chocolates.
- Bible story: Joseph has a cool coat and some incredible dreams. His brothers are jealous.

Day 2: The crime

Speak the truth!

- Opening talk: The police interview criminals separately to try to discover the truth.
- Puppet sketch: Bert commits a crime, giving his sister's picture to the guinea pig to chew—jealous again!
- Bible memory verse: I always speak the truth and refuse to tell a lie. (Proverbs 8:7)
- The Watt family: Grandma Watt, Rick and Wendy capture the robbers.
- Bible story: Joseph is sold into slavery.

Day 3: Falsely accused

Hold on tightly!

- Opening talk: The story of John's dad's minibus.
- Puppet sketch: The car wash: the inside of Dad's car gets soaked.
- Bible memory verse: We must hold tightly to the hope that we say is ours. After all, we can trust the one who made the agreement with us. (Hebrews 10:23)
- The Watt family: Grandma, Rick and Wendy are each framed for a crime and arrested.
- Bible story: Potiphar's wife tells lies about Joseph.

Day 4: Go to jail

And the jail-break to freedom!

- Opening talk: Road signs and the importance of rules.
- Puppet sketch: Football without rules leads to injury.
- Bible memory verse: Jesus said, 'If you keep on obeying what I have said, you truly are my disciples. You will know the truth, and the truth will set you free… If the Son gives you freedom, you are free!' (John 8:31–32, 36)
- The Watt family: Grandma, Rick and Wendy clear their names and hatch a plan.
- Bible story: Joseph interprets Pharaoh's dreams and is promoted to second in the kingdom.

Day 5: Forgiveness isn't easy

Hard choices

- Opening talk: The story of John and the ice cream trick.
- Puppet sketch: Lucy's friends forget to take her to the circus.
- Bible memory verse: Be kind and compassionate to one another, forgiving each other, just as in Christ God forgave you. (Ephesians 4:32, NIV)
- The Watt family: Showdown: the robbers get their come-uppance.
- Bible story: Joseph's brothers arrive, but have they really changed?

Theme song:
Cops & Robbers

Hello, hello, hello, what's going on here?

All the songs that accompany *The Cops & Robbers Holiday Club* are available from www.johnhardwick.org.uk. Visit YouTube and search for 'john hardwick org' to see the actions for the songs. Also, join the group 'Holiday Clubs and VBS by John Hardwick' on Facebook to hear stories, view images and get ideas about how other groups have used the material.

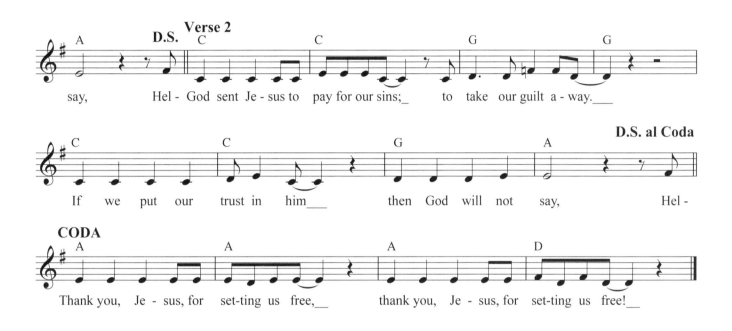

Reproduced with permission from *The Cops & Robbers Holiday Club* by John Hardwick,
published by Barnabas for Children 2014: www.barnabasinchurches.org.uk

The Watt family theme song

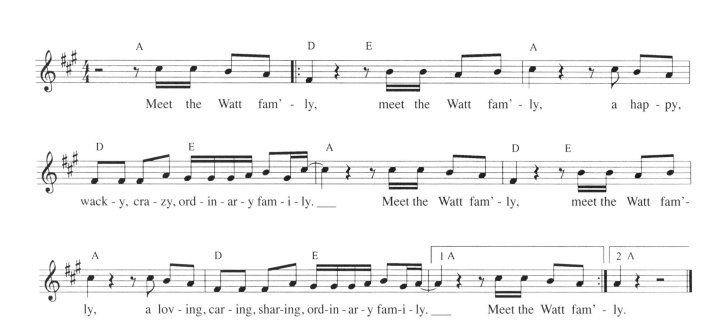

Reproduced with permission from *The Cops & Robbers Holiday Club* by John Hardwick,
published by Barnabas for Children 2014: www.barnabasinchurches.org.uk

The big Bible verse challenge

The Bible memory verses are based on the text of the Contemporary English Version or New International Version of the Bible. However, they do not necessarily include the whole verse, and the wording may vary slightly to fit the melody.

The memory verses can be turned into a big Bible verse challenge. Simply teach the verses, recap them each day and then challenge each team to see if they can remember them. This can be done during the quiz and also as a group time-filler. Even the youngest children can learn all five, and it is wonderful to hear them singing the verses spontaneously around the holiday club.

Please remember that, when using the songs during a holiday club, you are legally bound to include them on your CCL (Christian Copyright Licence). Speak to your church's music leader if you are unsure what this means.

Day 1: The plot

I know the plans I have for you
(Jeremiah 29:11, NIV)

Reproduced with permission from *The Cops & Robbers Holiday Club* by John Hardwick,
published by Barnabas for Children 2014: www.barnabasinchurches.org.uk

Day 2: The crime

Speak the truth! (Proverbs 8:7)

Reproduced with permission from *The Cops & Robbers Holiday Club* by John Hardwick,
published by Barnabas for Children 2014: www.barnabasinchurches.org.uk

Day 3: Falsely accused

Hold on tightly (Hebrews 10:23)

Day 4: Go to jail

Set free! (John 8:32, 36)

Day 5: Forgiveness isn't easy

Look in the Bible (Ephesians 4:32)

Be kind and com-pass-ion-ate to_____ one an-oth-er, be kind and com-pass-ion-ate to_____ one an-oth-er, for-give each oth-er, for-give each oth-er, just as in Christ God for-gave you._____ Be_____

Look in the Bi-ble, in the New Test-a-ment, Eph-es-ians four verse thir-ty-two.___ Look in the Bi-ble, in the New Test-a-ment, to find out what to_____ do!_____ Be

Opening talks

Each day there is a short opening talk to help set the scene and introduce the theme. The maximum length should be five minutes.

If you wish to make the talk more visual, you could download pictures or video clips from the internet to show the children what the police used to be like. Equally, you could use visual aids as appropriate (see suggestions below).

You could read the talk with plenty of enthusiasm, learn it by heart, tell it in your own words or make up a crib sheet with the key points. Whichever method you choose, please feel free to adapt the talks to suit your situation.

Day 1

The plot: Don't be jealous!

Cops and robbers, goodies and baddies, heroes and villains—all these themes dominate books, films and TV programmes.

Keystone Cops was a comical black-and-white silent movie series in the early days of cinema: see http://video.google.com/videoplay?docid=342544945856322429#

Dixon of Dock Green was a family television show that ran from 1955 to 1976 and had around 14 million viewers per episode. Ask your grandparents: they may have watched it when they were younger. Dixon of Dock Green was an old-fashioned ordinary copper (policeman) who would patrol his beat, stand underneath a blue police lamp and talk directly to the viewers. He'd often start by saying, 'Evening all', and then he would offer some sound and wise advice to the viewers, encouraging them to do the right things. There was a warm and safe feeling about Dixon of Dock Green. He was someone you could trust and rely on. Bobbies on the beat might say things like, 'Hello, hello—what's going on here?' or 'Let's be having you!'

You know, we wouldn't need police (cops) if we were perfect and did the right thing all the time. There would be no robbers, either. The world would be a wonderful place to live in. Sadly, many crimes are committed because we are jealous of what others have and often make bad choices. This week we're going to learn about a family in the Bible who made some bad choices and got into a terrible mess, but, thankfully, God sorted them out.

Day 2

The crime: Speak the truth!

Yippee! Often the cops catch the robbers, arrest them and take them to the police station. Then the police interview the robbers and ask them questions to try to discover the truth, but they don't interview the gang together. They split them up and interview them separately and record what they are saying. The robbers often lie to try to get out of trouble, and start blaming each other. But because the robbers don't know what each other has said, the police can often tell when they are lying and work out what really happened and who is to blame.

It's always best to tell the truth in the first place, because telling lies makes things much worse and no one can trust you any more.

Day 3

Falsely accused: Hold on tightly!

Have you ever been accused of doing something that you haven't done? It's horrible when no one will believe you. When this happens, it's important to hold on to what you know to be true and right.

This once happened to John, the writer of *The Cops & Robbers Holiday Club*. He says:

'When I was a young boy, my father drove a cream-and-green Bedford minibus. You didn't find many cream-and-green minibuses around. We needed a minibus because I was one of six children, and, with Mum and Dad too, that made eight of us in the family.

'One day when I was very young, I remember my father driving along in our cream-and-green minibus when suddenly a police car pulled alongside us with its blue lights flashing and its siren blaring. The policeman ordered Dad to pull over and stop. Dad did as he was told. All six of us children watched to see what was happening and could just about overhear what was being said. The policeman said to my dad, "We believe you have been involved in a bank robbery. This cream-and-green minibus is the get-away vehicle."

'My father was amazed and said, "When was this exactly?"

'"This morning," came the policeman's reply.

'"We've had a family outing today. I think you have the wrong man and minibus," said Dad.

'"I think we'll be the judge of that," said the policeman in a harsh voice, and the conversation continued.

'My dad became a bit cross and said, "Do you really think I would rob a bank with all my family in the car?" The policeman looked and saw all our little faces staring at him. "Do they look like a gang of hardened criminals?" continued my dad.

'"We'll let you go for now, but we will send an officer round to see you later." And they did!'

John's father had been falsely accused of a crime he hadn't committed. Later, we are going to hear about a story in which Joseph is accused of a terrible crime.

Jesus was falsely accused but chose to take the punishment for our sins.

Day 4

Go to jail: And the jail-break to freedom!

Why are rules important? Surely we would all be much happier if there were no laws or rules.

Show a few road signs and see if the children know what they mean:

- A 40 miles per hour road sign
- A warning sign: coming up to a sharp bend
- Traffic lights

What could happen if we chose to ignore these road signs? People would get hurt, maybe even lose their life or take someone else's.

Rules are there for a reason. God gives his laws for a reason, but often we disobey God's rules and wonder why the world is in a mess. Later we are going to hear a story about two people. One wanted to break one of God's rules, while the other one chose to keep God's rule.

Day 5

Forgiveness isn't easy: Hard choices

John, the writer of *The Cops & Robbers Holiday Club*, tells the story of when he was a boy and playing in the park with some friends:

'It was a really hot day and suddenly an ice cream van pulled up. My friends quickly joined the queue and bought their ice creams. I dug deep into my pockets and found just about enough money for an ice cream. By the time I had bought my ice cream, my friends had finished theirs, and one of them said, "Hey, John, does your ice cream smell like it's gone bad?" I immediately put my nose to my ice cream to smell it, and, as I did so, my friends pushed the ice cream up into my face. They thought this was a very funny joke and laughed and laughed, but I didn't. I was really looking forward to enjoying my ice cream, I'd had to queue for a long time to get it, and spent all my money, and then they had ruined it by pushing it in my face so that most of the ice cream fell on the ground.'

Has anything like that ever happened to you? What would you do?

When John's friends finally stopped laughing, they could see on his face how upset he was. It hadn't been very funny after all: they had hurt a good friend, and thankfully they were real mates and said 'sorry'. John then had a hard choice to make—to forgive or not to forgive. He chose to forgive them, and those friends remained his friends for many years to come.

Later we are going to hear about a hard choice that Joseph had to make—whether or not to forgive some people who had tried to get rid of him for ever and ruin his life.

Jesus was nailed to the cross and left to die. He hadn't done anything to deserve this—but do you know what some of Jesus' last words were before he died? Today we are looking at why forgiving others is so, so important.

Theme illustrations and challenges

The plot: Don't be jealous!

Ask for two older child volunteers. Witnesses to a crime need to remember what they have seen and heard. Let's see how observant our volunteers are.

Bring out a 'dodgy-looking character'. The volunteers have 30 seconds to look at them and try to remember their appearance. They also need to listen to what the dodgy-looking character is saying, as they will be asked questions. (Deliberately ask simpler questions to your first volunteer and much harder questions to your second volunteer.)

Have your character wearing big thick glasses, a hat and long trousers so that you cannot see their socks.

The character could say something like this: 'It can't have been me, officer. I was in the pub from 7.53 to 9.38pm with two mates, Jake Reynolds and Ben Mustow.'

Ask questions about your character's appearance:

- To first volunteer: Was our dodgy-looking character wearing glasses or not? *(Yes)*
- To second volunteer: What colour socks was he/she wearing? *(Of course they won't know the answer because they couldn't see the socks)*
- To first volunteer: Was he/she wearing a hat? *(Yes)*
- To second volunteer: Was he/she hiding anything in the hat? *(Of course they won't know the answer)*

Ask questions about what your character said:

- To first volunteer: Where did our dodgy-looking character say he had been? *(The pub)*

- To second volunteer: What time did he/she say he/she was there? *(7.53–9.38pm)*
- To first volunteer: Was he/she with some mates? *(Yes)*
- To second volunteer: What were their names? *(Jake Reynolds and Ben Mustow)*

Your first volunteer will probably have answered all their questions correctly, whereas your second volunteer will have struggled to answer any correctly. Give the first volunteer a prize, and nothing to the second volunteer.

Send the first volunteer back to their place, but ask the second volunteer what they thought of the questions. Did they think the questions were fair? How did they feel when the first volunteer received a prize and they did not? Your second volunteer will probably have felt jealous or hard-done-by.

Sometimes life isn't fair. How do we react when other people seem to get more than we do and are treated better than us? Later we are going to hear a story about some brothers who were not treated fairly at all. I wonder how they reacted.

The crime: Speak the truth!

When the police catch a suspect (someone they think may have committed a crime), they ask the suspect questions. Sometimes the suspect was not involved in the crime and is innocent, so they tell a true story. Other times, though, the suspect did commit the crime but doesn't want the police to find out, so they make up a story. The police need to find out who is telling the truth and who is telling a lie.

Carry out a 'Truth or lie' test (based on 'True or false'). You'll need to ask the leaders to tell you some unusual true-life stories that they are prepared to share with the children. Also ask some of the leaders to make up a story that is completely untrue. Have six leaders with stories—three with a true story and three with made-up stories.

Ask for a volunteer from each team who doesn't mind getting a bit messy. (It may be best to choose children just from the older teams.) Sit the volunteers down on chairs and ask the six leaders to tell their stories in turn to the volunteers. The volunteers listen to each story and have to decide whether the leader is telling the truth or a lie. If the volunteer makes the right choice, they receive a prize (such as a sweet), but if they get it wrong they receive a custard pie or similar punishment.

An example story could be: 'When I was a girl, I went to boarding school. One day I stole the head teacher's underwear from the washing line and flew it on the school flagpole.' Is this leader telling the truth or is it a made-up story—a lie?

My true story would be: 'When I (John Hardwick) had my stag do, my so-called mates grabbed me, put my arm in a plaster cast, stole my clothes (just leaving me with a grass skirt), drove me down to London, pushed me out of the car outside the Houses of Parliament, left me with my unicycle and told me to cycle home. This was bad enough, but my best man is now the Head of Missions for Scripture Union!'

People who constantly tell lies soon find out that no one trusts them. Even when they do tell the truth, no one will believe them. Isn't it sad if no one knows whether they can believe you or not? Let's do our best to tell the truth, and don't give in to the temptation to tell a lie or cheat in a test.

Later we're going to hear a story about some people who committed a terrible crime and told an even worse lie to try to cover their tracks.

Day 3

Falsely accused: Hold on tightly!

Set up a simple obstacle course around the edge of the room (not too many obstacles or it will take too long). Ask for six volunteers and invite them to hold on to a piece of rope. The idea is that the children hold on to the same piece of rope as they move through the course. It may be difficult to keep holding on, as the children at the front may be moving so quickly that those at the back can't keep up, so encourage them to work as a team by talking and listening to each other and setting the right pace. Those who make it to the end of the obstacle course without letting go of the rope will receive a small prize.

Also, on the way, include some leaders who are primed to tempt the volunteers off the course. They may falsely accuse them of cheating even though they know they have not done so, or they may tempt them with extra prizes—but can they be trusted? The volunteers need to hold on tightly and keep going to receive the prize at the end of the course.

Later we'll hear a story about someone who was tempted to do something wrong, but this person was determined to 'hold on tightly' to follow God's laws, even though it meant being accused of something he didn't do. When we choose to do what God wants us to do, it doesn't mean we'll have an easy life. Sometimes people try to tempt us to do wrong things and, if we don't follow their suggestions, they may choose to fall out with us. We need to hold on tightly to God and keep following his ways.

Day 4

Go to jail: And the jail-break to freedom!

Bring out a 'tough guy' leader (briefed beforehand). Ask them if they think they are tough enough to break a piece of cotton. Now let them prove it: tie their two wrists together with a single piece of cotton thread, then ask the tough guy to snap the cotton and break free. (They should be able to do this quite easily by pulling their wrists apart.)

Sometimes people may do something wrong but they think, 'Oh well, that doesn't matter, I'm sure God won't mind!' But God does mind and he wants us to confess and say 'sorry' to him even for the small things. Let me show you why.

Wrap the cotton around the wrists of the tough guy volunteer again (keeping it tight on their wrists), but not just once. Keep wrapping it round as you say things like the suggestions below. (You may wish to practise with the tough guy beforehand to work out how many times you need to wrap the cotton around their wrists before they can no longer break free. Remember to keep it tight.)

'As I've already said, sometimes we think that the small things we do wrong don't really matter, but they do.

'Let's say [name the leader] tells a little white lie. No harm there, surely! Let's wrap the cotton round his wrists a few times to represent the little white lie. I'm sure he could still break free if he wanted.

'But let's say one day he loses his temper with someone and starts shouting and even swearing at them. Well, at least he didn't hit them, so there's no real harm done—or is there? Let's wrap the cotton round his wrists a few more times to represent him losing his temper.

'Maybe one day his brother or sister or friend really annoys him, so he pinches them and makes them upset. Surely no real harm done—or is there? Let's wrap the cotton around his wrists a few more times.

'Maybe he sees something in a shop that he knows he can't afford, but it's easy to slip it into his pocket without anyone noticing. I'm sure it won't be missed—no real harm done—or is there? Let's wrap the cotton around the wrists another few times.

'None of these crimes or wrongs—the Bible calls them 'sins'—seems very bad, but look what happens. [Ask the tough guy to snap the thread and break free: now they are unable to do so.] See how one sin leads to another and before long we are trapped. You need someone else to come along and set you free. [Cut the tough guy loose.] When Jesus died on the cross, it was as if he was cutting us free. Even though Jesus did nothing wrong, he loved us so much that he died on the cross for the wrong things we have done, breaking the hold that our sin has on us.'

Day 5

Forgiving isn't easy: Hard choices

Choose two volunteers (preferably from the 8–10 age group) who are about the same weight and of a similar strength. (For the purpose of illustration, I'll call them Jack and Jill.) Jack and Jill stand facing each other, both holding on to a dog's 'tug-of-war' rubber ring with one hand. Ask one leader to stand about two metres behind Jack, holding a bowl with three sweets, and another leader to stand about two metres behind Jill, holding a bowl with three sweets. Jack and Jill must use their free hands to reach behind them to grab sweets from the bowls.

Tell Jack and Jill that they have 30 seconds to get as many sweets as possible out of their own bowl, one at a time. When they have taken one, they have to move right back to the centre before trying to get another.

The volunteers will automatically think that this means it's a tug-of-war and will pull against each other. The 30 seconds will pass very quickly and Jack and Jill will struggle to get even one of their sweets, let alone all three.

Tell them that it would have been possible for both Jack and Jill to get all three sweets. How? If Jack and Jill move in the same direction together, the goal can be achieved. Let the two volunteers try again, this time working together and travelling in the same direction.

It's impossible for us human beings to go through life without making mistakes and hurting one another. Some people think that the answer is to get away from everyone. If they go through life on their own, then they won't get hurt—but they will also miss out on a lot of happiness. The real answer is learning how to forgive and love one another so that we can move along together in the same direction. We also need to ask God to show us his way forward. But forgiving isn't easy.

Later we're going to hear about someone who needed to forgive some people, but it proved to be the hardest thing ever.

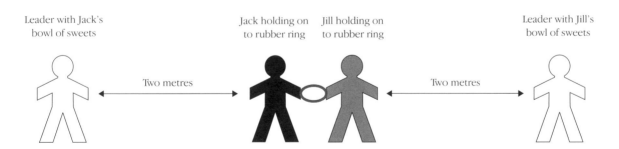

Leader with Jack's bowl of sweets   Jack holding on to rubber ring   Jill holding on to rubber ring   Leader with Jill's bowl of sweets

Two metres   Two metres

The Watt family daily dramas: Cops & Robbers adventure

The daily drama picks up the main themes of the holiday club but is given a light-hearted touch, with the intention of providing a fun-filled dramatic interlude rather than a serious teaching point. Children love the different characters and can't wait for the next adventure the following day, making the serial drama formula an incentive for them to attend each holiday club.

Drama tips

Many of the following drama tips are also useful for those telling the Bible narrations.

- A minimum of six one-hour rehearsals is recommended, so you will need to start rehearsing about six weeks before the holiday club. The rehearsals should be fun and provide a good way for members of the team to get to know each other better. The first rehearsal will involve casting the drama and reading through the whole script to get into the storyline. You may choose to record this read-through and make copies for each member of the cast. This is a good technique for learning lines quickly.

- Project your voice: speak out loud and clear. Don't turn your back to the audience when speaking. It is better to face the audience and turn your head to the side when speaking to another character. For open expression, point one foot towards the character you are speaking to and the other foot towards the audience.

- A technician can be useful. Background music or sound effects can add to the atmosphere, but don't make them so loud that the actors can't be heard.

- If you are playing the part of a baddie, try to be a nice, cheeky baddie, rather than a very loud, aggressive one. Little children scare easily.

- Don't rush lines. Often, jokes are lost because the delivery isn't clear. The Watt family scripts have been designed to be short and easy to learn, but you need to make the characters come to life through plenty of movement. It is useful if someone with experience in drama can come to your rehearsals to watch and direct you in the delivery of lines and stage blocking. Constructive criticism can help to bring the drama to life.

- Think about movement and facial expression, entrances and exits. If there is a chase scene, work out a routine and decide whether you need to have some 'chase' music playing in the background. Often, children find this type of humour funnier than the actual lines.

- Think about your set and costumes: don't leave costumes and props to the last minute. Don't forget your local toyshop and costume shop in your search for costumes and props, but try the internet, too. For example, sites such as www.hawkin.com can provide bubble blower guns (ideal for Rick), www. partybox.co.uk supplies wigs and costumes, and www.sound-effects-library.com offers a full range of sound effect CDs.

If you are struggling to find budding actors to perform the Watt family adventure, the story can be read straight from the script, using plenty of expression. Alternatively, a recording of the script is available on John's website, www.johnhardwick.org.uk. To encourage children to listen, ask two leaders to look out for the best listeners, who will earn extra points for their team (or a prize token).

Day 1: The plot

Main characters
- Narrator: A competent leader to introduce and round off the story each day
- Grandma Watt: A wacky fun-loving character, who always has a walking stick with her as part of her costume
- Rick Watt: A fun-loving, action-packed boy
- Wendy Watt: Rick's big sister. She's a little bossy and talks a lot
- Two robbers in stripy shirts, with tights over their faces and wearing masks

Props
A drink; a water pistol; a box of chocolates; a robber's swag bag

Play the Watt family theme tune and encourage the children to sing along. Use this time to get the props and actors in position.

Narrator:	Grandma does not look happy! She is obviously looking for something.
Wendy:	*(Sipping a drink, then notices the audience)* Hello, everyone! *(Very quickly, all in one breath)* I'm Wendy Watt, they say I talk a lot but I don't really talk a lot, I only talk if nobody is talking, then I may as well talk. Grandma is being all grumpy!
Grandma:	Put a sock in it, Wendy!
Wendy:	What, in my drink?
Grandma:	No, your mouth, dear! *(To audience)* I'm Grandma Watt, and I suppose I am a bit grumpy because…
Rick:	*(Comes on shooting his water pistol like James Bond)* And I'm Watt, Rick Watt. I'm cool and crazy!
Wendy:	He thinks he's James Bond.
Grandma:	Rick, do be quiet. Can't you see I'm being all grumpy and trying to think?
Rick:	*(Excitedly)* That's not like you, Grandma!
Grandma:	What, being grumpy?
Rick:	No, the 'trying to think' bit.
Grandma:	Watch it!
Rick:	Sorry, did you say 'stink' or 'think'?

Grandma:	Oi! Watch it, you!
Rick:	Why are you all grumpy, then?
Grandma:	Because a terrible crime has been committed.
Wendy:	*(Looks shocked)* Oh dear. What terrible crime, Grandma?
Grandma:	Was it you, Rick? I want to know—who's done it?
Rick:	What?
Grandma:	Who committed the terrible crime? Was it you, Rick?
Rick:	*(Nodding with a smirk)* Probably! *(Then shakes his head)* Actually, it wasn't me! I'm not the guilty one, I'm a good boy!

Both Grandma and Wendy look at Rick with shocked expressions.

Rick:	I'm telling the truth! I have been a good boy, for a change.
Wendy:	Come on, Grandma, tell us—what terrible crime has been committed?

Grandma produces a box of chocolates from behind her back and opens it.

Grandma:	Someone has eaten all the strawberry cream chocolates.
Rick:	*(Looks disappointed)* Oh, is that all? I thought a real crime had been committed.
Wendy:	Actually, Rick, did you know that somewhere in the world right now, a terrible crime is being committed? And robbers sometimes even break into people's homes and steal things even when the home owners are still there.
Grandma:	Thanks. That's really cheered me up.
Rick:	Wow, Wendy! How do you know?
Wendy:	It's a well-known fact.
Rick:	Ha! How silly! Fancy not realising that robbers are stealing things out of your house even when you are there.

As he is talking, two robbers sneak up on tiptoe behind them and start putting items in their bag. One of them even reaches around Grandma, sneaks a chocolate out of the box and puts it in his mouth.

Robber 1:	Thank you!
Grandma:	*(Not realising what she is saying)* My pleasure, dear.

The Watt family are so busy talking, they still don't realise that robbers are stealing from them. Hopefully the audience will soon tell them. If they do not, plant someone to say:

Audience:	Robbers!
Watt family:	Robbers? Where?
Audience:	Behind you!

The Watt family all slowly turn around in a clockwise direction. As they do so, the robbers also creep round in a clockwise direction so that the family can't see them. They turn all the way around so that they are facing the audience, with the robbers behind them again.

Rick:	I didn't see anyone.
Wendy:	Nor me.
Grandma:	Me neither.
Audience:	They're behind you!

This time the Watt family spin around quickly and see the robbers. Play some chase music and work out a chase routine. The robbers then run off stage with the Watt family close behind.

Narrator:	Oh dear, the Watt family appear to have been robbed. Did they steal all of Grandma's strawberry creams… or was that Rick? Find out in the next exciting episode of the Watt family Cops & Robbers adventure.

Play Watt family theme tune.

Day 2: The crime

Main characters
- Narrator
- Grandma Watt
- Rick Watt
- Wendy Watt

Props
A piece of paper with a shoe print on it; a mobile phone

Narrator:	Oh dear, yesterday the Watt family were visited by some robbers. Although the Watt family put up a chase, the robbers made a clean getaway.
Grandma:	It wasn't exactly clean. They left mud all over the floor—and that's their first mistake, isn't it, Rick?
Rick:	Yes, their first mistake.
Wendy:	Rick, do you know what Grandma is going on about?
Rick:	No, but it sounds good.
Wendy:	*(Sees a muddy footprint on the floor)* Oh dear, the robbers didn't wipe their feet and have left a muddy footprint on the floor.
Grandma:	Yes, what good luck!
Rick:	What? I get told off if I forget to wipe my feet.
Grandma:	Look. I have a piece of paper.

Grandma puts the piece of paper on the floor on top of the footprint, and, as she picks it up, a shoe print can be seen on the paper.

Wendy:	Clever stuff, Grandma!
Grandma:	*(Pointing)* Looks like a size 9 boot, with dents in the tread just there and there. We can identify the boot from this, as no two treads on a boot are exactly the same.
Wendy:	Wow, Grandma—you're like Sherlock Holmes.
Rick:	Is that an estate agent?
Grandma:	And did you notice they were wearing tights over their faces?
Wendy:	Yes. Now we'll never know who they are.
Grandma:	Their second mistake!
Rick:	Mistake? How come?

Reproduced with permission from *The Cops & Robbers Holiday Club* by John Hardwick, published by Barnabas for Children 2014: www.barnabasinchurches.org.uk

Grandma:	They were no ordinary pair of tights. They were *(in an over-dramatic TV advert voice)* M&S support tights. My friend Mabel had two pairs of M&S support tights stolen from her washing line only yesterday. She had bare legs all day.
Rick:	*(Pulls a face)* Too much information, Grandma!
Grandma:	There were some footprints near her line, so she made a copy, like we did.
Rick:	*(Astonished)* Wow!
Grandma:	With no time to lose, she followed the trail, which led to her neighbour's house. She reckons the print belongs to one of the men who lives next door to her.
Wendy:	You old girls never cease to amaze me.
Grandma:	*(Taking her mobile phone out of her bag)* Yo, Mabel? Grandma Watt here. Did you scan in the boot print? Great, attach it to an email and send it to me. We also have a boot print—if they match, we have the culprit. Actually, no need, just take a photo of the boot print and send it to my phone.
Rick:	Grandma, you really are so cool!
Grandma:	*(Still on the phone)* Yes, Mabel, I've received it and it's a match—the same boot print. Contact the girls, we're going in!
Wendy:	'Contact the girls, we're going in'? Grandma, don't you think you ought to tell the police and let them sort it out?
Grandma:	Yes, you're right. *(To Mabel)* Send the picture to our usual contact at the Met. *(To Wendy)* Good thinking, Wendy. *(Back to phone)* Oh dear, the police are out on a job already. It's up to us— we need to catch them red-handed. Come on!

Rick and Wendy excitedly follow Grandma off to stage right. The two robbers enter stage left—not wearing tights over their faces.

Robber 1:	It's been a good day today.
Robber 2:	Yes, very pleasant day for robbing.
Robber 1:	We've got loads of stuff.
Robber 2:	And some strawberry cream chocolate.
Robber 1:	And that fake bank robbery did the trick by sending the police off in the wrong direction.

Robber 2:	Yeah, we got clean away. I'm pleased we've taken off those tights—they were awfully… tight.

Wendy suddenly appears in front of the robbers. As soon as she starts to speak, Rick sneaks up and ties the robbers' shoelaces together.

Wendy:	*(To the robbers, extra quickly)* Excuse me, have you got the time please, it would be great if you have because I don't want to be home late for tea. Actually, those are our chocolates. *(She snatches them and runs off)*

The Watt family sneak up behind the robbers. Grandma hooks her walking stick around their feet without them noticing. The robbers try to chase Wendy but fall to the ground, and Grandma sits on them.

Robber 1:	It's a fair cop, cop!
Robber 2:	It would be if that was a copper.
Grandma:	You mean 'policeman'.
Robber 1:	Er, thank you, yes—policeman. *(To Robber 2)* What do you mean?
Robber 2:	Look—it's not a policeman. It's an old lady and two little children that have captured us.
Robber 1:	What? Get them! *(Both robbers struggle to get away)*
Narrator:	Can the Watt family hold the robbers until the police get there? Have the strawberry creams been squashed by now? You'll have to find out in the next exciting episode of the Watt family Cops & Robbers adventure.

Play Watt family theme tune.

Reproduced with permission from *The Cops & Robbers Holiday Club* by John Hardwick, published by Barnabas for Children 2014: www.barnabasinchurches.org.uk

Main characters
- Narrator
- Grandma Watt
- Rick Watt
- Wendy Watt

Other cast members
- The Big Bad Boss
- Jogger
- Shopper
- Business person
- PC BobUpAndDown

Props

A mobile phone; an iPod; a shopping bag; a brief-case, a police radio or phone

Narrator: If you remember, we left Grandma Watt sitting on some robbers that she and the children had just captured— but the robbers were trying to get away. Did the Watt family manage to hold on?

Wendy: Yes, thankfully, we phoned the police, who arrived very quickly. They came along and arrested the two robbers. In fact, you only just missed them. They've just gone.

Grandma: It was a bit disappointing, really. I was hoping we could go in the police car too and have a trip with the lights flashing and siren screaming.

Rick: Yeah, that would have been cool, but they couldn't fit us in with the robbers.

Grandma: So the robbers got a lift and we have to walk.

Rick: Walking's good for you, Grandma. And I can shoot all the birds with my water pistol.

Wendy: Don't you dare!

They walk off, stage right. Criminal mastermind, the Big Bad Boss, enters stage left, talking on his mobile phone.

Big Bad Boss: What do you mean, my robbers have been arrested? The plan was perfect. We set up a fake bank robbery so that all the police would rush to the bank, leaving our top robbers to do the robbing. So what went wrong? *(Looks surprised)* Sorry, can you say that again? I thought you said they were caught by a little old lady who sat on them. *(Slight pause while listening)* You did say they were caught by a little old lady who sat on them—but she had back-up. Who? *(Listens again; shouts into the phone)* You call a little boy and a loud-mouthed girl 'back-up'? *(A bit calmer)* Did you get the name of this grandma and kids? I'll teach them to mess with me! *(Pause while listening)* Who? *(Listens)* Not who but what? What are you going on about? *(Listens)* Oh, Watt is their name. Grandma Watt, Rick Watt and Wendy Watt—the famous Watt family!

Big Bad Boss suddenly looks up and sees the audience.

Big Bad Boss: *(To audience)* Oh, hello—I didn't see you. I'm the Boss—sometimes called the Big Bad Boss, but I really don't know why. I hope you didn't overhear my conversation? You did? Oh dear! Well, I'd better go, because I've had an idea. It's a very good idea. In fact, it's a very, very good idea that will get rid of that menacing Watt family once and for all. You'll see! *(Walking slowly off, stage left)* Genius—I'm a genius!

A jogger wearing an iPod comes on and jogs around the stage. Grandma Watt, wearing dark shades or a mask, enters and starts to chase the jogger around the stage in a figure of eight. You could include some chase music. Finally Grandma manages to trip the jogger with her walking stick, steals the jogger's iPod and runs off stage. The jogger is left on the ground crying.

Next, a person with a bag of shopping walks on to the stage. Rick Watt, wearing dark shades or a mask, runs on stage and shoots his water pistol at the person carrying the shopping bag. The person drops the bag and Rick picks it up and runs off with it, leaving the person sobbing, 'How can I feed my family now?'

Finally, a business man or woman walks on stage, carrying a briefcase. Wendy Watt, wearing dark shades or a mask, enters and steps in front of the business person, who stops. Wendy points upwards and the business person looks up. Wendy tickles the business person's ribs and they start laughing and

Reproduced with permission from *The Cops & Robbers Holiday Club* by John Hardwick, published by Barnabas for Children 2014: www.barnabasinchurches.org.uk

drop the briefcase. Wendy picks up the briefcase and runs around the stage, with the business person trying to catch her. Finally the business person is exhausted, stops chasing, and Wendy runs off stage with the briefcase.

A police officer walks on stage and sees the three victims.

PC: Morning, all! *(Bobbing up and down)* Hello, hello, hello, hello. What's going on here?

Jogger: I've been robbed by an old lady, who stole my iPod. Although she was wearing a mask, I know exactly who it was. It was Grandma Watt.

Narrator: Dum, dum, dum!

PC: Oh dear, oh dear! *(To the shopper)* And what's going on here?

Shopper: I've been robbed by a young boy, who stole my shopping. How will I feed my family now? The boy was wearing a mask, but I know exactly who it was. It was Rick Watt.

Narrator: Dum, dum, dum!

PC: Oh dear, oh dear! *(To the business person)* And what's going on here?

Business person: I've been robbed by a girl, who tickled my ribs and stole my briefcase. Although she was wearing a mask, I know exactly who it was. It was Wendy Watt.

Narrator: Dum, dum, dum!

PC: *(To narrator)* Will you stop going 'Dum, dum, dum'? It's very annoying. I need to make a call through to the station. *(On radio or phone)* Hello, hello, hello, it's PC BobUpAndDown here. *(Bobs up and down)* I'm afraid the Watt family have turned bad. They need to be arrested at once. Over and out.

Narrator: Oh no! Have the Watt family turned bad? What was the Big Bad Boss's wicked plan to get rid of them? Find out in the next exciting episode of the Watt family Cops & Robbers adventure.

Play Watt family theme tune.

Day 4: Go to jail

Main characters
- Narrator
- Grandma Watt
- Rick Watt
- Wendy Watt

Other cast members
- PC BobUpAndDown
- The Big Bad Boss
- Detective
- Police extras

Props
A police radio or phone; a water pistol; chase music

Narrator: Oh no, it looks as if the famous Watt family have turned bad. The police have just turned up at the Watt family's house and are arresting them. Let's listen carefully so that we know what's going on.

PC: *(On radio or phone)* Yes, Sergeant, I've just arrived at Number 5 Letsby Avenue.

Grandma: Oh, it's nice to see you, PC BobUpAndDown. *(He bobs up and down)* I'm so pleased you called around. Would you like a nice cup of tea? I've got some important news I need to tell you.

PC: I have no time for a nice chat or a cup of tea with you. I have come to arrest you and your grandchildren. We are very disappointed in you all. You are role models and should set a good example, but what you did yesterday was a terrible thing.

Rick: Cool! Does that mean we get to go in the police car with lights flashing and siren screaming?

Grandma: Oh, that will be fun.

Wendy: Er, I don't think you have taken in what PC BobUpAndDown *(he bobs up and down)* said. We're under arrest.

Grandma: We're under a vest? Don't be silly, Wendy!

PC: It's true—you are under a vest. *(Realises what he has said)* I mean, arrest. Now come with me.

Rick:	Yippee! We're going in a police car with lights flashing and the siren screaming.
PC:	I'm afraid all the other police cars have been called away to a bank robbery…
Grandma:	(*Interrupting*) What, again?
PC:	… so I'm on my bicycle. You'll have to walk.
Rick:	(*Disappointed*) Oh! (*Looks brighter*) Has it got a bell? Can I have a ding?
Grandma:	Can I go on the back of the bicycle? That will be fun.
PC:	No, that's against the law. You have to walk.

All walk off, stage right. The Big Bad Boss enters stage left, dancing around for joy.

Big Bad Boss:	(*Excitedly*) It worked, it worked! I've got that menacing Watt family out of the way. And now all the police have gone to another hoax call about a bank robbery while my robbers are doing some more robbing. I'm such a mastermind criminal—no one is as clever as me, and no one can stop me with the Watt family out of the way. Ha, ha, ha…

Audience boo as the Big Bad Boss exits stage left. The Watt family enter stage right, arriving in the interview room at the police station.

Detective:	Well, Watts, what is going on? What's going on, I say? What have you got to say for yourself, Watts? What, what?
Grandma:	Why so many whats?
Detective:	What?
Wendy:	Don't say 'what', say 'pardon'! But I've worked it out.
Detective:	What?
Wendy:	What's going on. It wasn't us who did those terrible things yesterday. We've been falsely accused. Remember, yesterday, Grandma, you had some clothes stolen off the line. Well, so did Rick and I, and Rick said…
Rick:	It's as if someone wants to pretend to be us.
Grandma:	Exactly.
Detective:	What?
Grandma:	I received a phone call saying that some robbers were targeting our street again and telling me not to go out.
Detective:	What? (*Suddenly dawns on him*) Oh, I get it. Someone wants you out of the way so badly that they stole your clothes… then robbed those people while pretending to be you… so they had to keep the real Watt family out of the way… which is why they phoned you telling you to stay in.
Rick:	Good detective work, Detective!
Detective:	Thank you! We're been after this gang of robbers for ages, but with your help I think I have a plan to catch them which might just work. It could be dangerous, but are you willing to give it a try?
Rick:	Dangerous is my middle name.
Grandma:	I thought it was James, Rick.
Rick:	It is, but… oh, never mind. What do you want us to do?
Detective:	It's a game of 'Let's pretend'.
Wendy:	Sounds fun.
Detective:	I'm going to pretend to accuse you, the Watt family, of being the mastermind behind all these crimes. As I do, I want you to pretend to try to escape. You need to make it realistic, otherwise no one will believe us.
Wendy:	This is so exciting!
Detective:	I will then let the press know that…
Rick:	(*Interrupting*) Press?
Detective:	… the newspapers, radio and television… that you are wanted criminals who are responsible not only for the crimes in this town but in many others. The real mastermind criminal won't like you taking all the credit and will come after you. When he does, we'll catch him and his gang.
Grandma:	No! Too dangerous! You've worked out that we are innocent, so just let us go.
Detective:	Yes, sorry, Grandma. You're right, what was I thinking? You are free to go.
Wendy:	But Grandma, don't you remember how upset you were when you realised someone had stolen your chocolate strawberry creams?
Grandma:	What's that got to do with it?
Wendy:	Well, people have had some really precious items stolen—things that they have worked hard to buy—and now they are really upset.
Rick:	Yes, it's wrong to steal from other people and take what doesn't belong

Reproduced with permission from *The Cops & Robbers Holiday Club* by John Hardwick, published by Barnabas for Children 2014: www.barnabasinchurches.org.uk

to you. We have a chance to help the police catch them. What do you say, Grandma?

Grandma suddenly takes Rick's water pistol and shoots it into the detective's face.

Detective: Yuck!
Grandma: Catch me if you can!

Play some chase music (such as the Benny Hill theme tune) and have as many police as you can running after the Watt family, up and down the hall, round and round the stage, until eventually all exit.

Narrator: Well, the police are chasing the Watt family, but are they really? Will it really fool the Big Bad Boss and his gang of criminals? Find out in the next exciting episode of the Watt family Cops & Robbers adventure.

Play Watt family theme tune.

Main characters
- Narrator
- Grandma Watt
- Rick Watt
- Wendy Watt

Other cast members
- Detective and police extras
- The Big Bad Boss
- Two robbers

Props
Chase music; 'James Bond' background music (optional); two mobile phones

Narrator: Welcome back. In our last exciting episode, the police were all chasing the Watt family.

Continue the chase from yesterday, playing the same music, with the police running after the Watt family, up and down the hall and round and round the stage. The Watt family run off stage again, but the police slow down and look out of breath. They give up the chase and stagger off stage. The Big Bad Boss and the two robbers enter.

Big Bad Boss: I don't believe it! The Watt family have taken all the credit, all the glory for my crimes. *(Getting upset)* I'm the criminal mastermind, not Grandma Watt! It's not fair—boo hoo!
Robber 1: Don't cry, boss. We still think you're the best criminal mastermind, even if no one else does.
Robber 2: Yeah! You are definitely the meanest, most uncaring person I have ever met.
Big Bad Boss: Thanks for trying to cheer me up, guys.
Robber 1: *(Arms wide)* Group hug!
Robber 2: Yeah!
Big Bad Boss: *(Interrupts angrily)* No! I can't believe I just said 'thank you'. I never use words like that. And as for a group hug, have you forgotten that we are the bad guys? Now let's go and catch the Watt family and show them that I'm the Big Bad Boss around here and I want no more of this mushy stuff. Group hug, indeed! Actually... you

Reproduced with permission from *The Cops & Robbers Holiday Club* by John Hardwick, published by Barnabas for Children 2014: www.barnabasinchurches.org.uk

42

	two find them and report back to me, because I'm going home for a rest. All this criminal masterminding is very tiring.
Narrator:	Who is that hiding there? It's the Watt family. I don't believe it, they've found the Big Bad Boss and are following him. Be careful, Watt family!

The Big Bad Boss walks along, the Watt family creeping quietly along behind him with fingers to lips. Play some background music such as the James Bond theme tune. The Big Bad Boss walks off stage. The Watt family pause.

Wendy	*(To Grandma, in a stage whisper)* Psst! What's the plan, Grandma? Are we planning to break into his house and tie him up, then smash up his belongings, like his gang do when they break into people's homes?
Grandma:	Oh no!
Rick:	OK, then, are we going to steal his precious belongings so that he becomes sad, like the people his gang steal from?
Grandma:	Oh no!
Rick:	But why not? After all, that's what he does to everyone else. He doesn't care, so why should anyone care about him?
Grandma:	That's revenge, and we would be just as bad as he is if we did that to him. No, we'll just tell the police where he is and leave them to sort him out.

The robbers and the Big Bad Boss run back on stage. Play some chase music as the two robbers chase after Rick, round and round the stage. Suddenly Rick stops and points upwards.

Rick:	Look!

Robber 1 looks up. Rick darts between his legs, causing him to lose his balance. Robber 2 goes to help and Rick gives him a gentle push, knocking him straight on top of Robber 1. Grandma and Wendy give a big cheer, but the Big Bad Boss sneaks up behind Rick and grabs hold of him.

Big Bad Boss:	Grandma and Wendy Watt, give up or Rick gets it!
Wendy:	Gets what—an ice cream?
Robber 1:	Yum! Can I have one too?
Big Bad Boss:	*(Snaps)* No, you can't. Don't mess with me!

Grandma:	OK, we give in. Don't hurt him.
Big Bad Boss:	Oh, I don't hurt people. I get my robber gang to do it for me.
Rick:	That's the same thing. If you get others to hurt people for you, then you're an even bigger coward than they are.
Big Bad Boss:	I'm not a coward. I'm a criminal mastermind.
Rick:	You are not. You break into people's homes.
Wendy:	Why don't you get a proper job, rather than ruining other people's lives?
Big Bad Boss:	Ruin people's lives? I do not. I just steal things, that's all. What's the harm in that? They can always buy some more.
Grandma:	You are a hard man and only care about yourself.

The Big Bad Boss's phone rings.

Big Bad Boss:	Excuse me, it's the boss on the phone.
Robbers:	We thought you were the boss!
Big Bad Boss:	Er, yes, I am, but it's my wife. *(Listens)* What? No! It can't be! What's been taken? No… *(Starts to cry)* Boo hoo!
Robber 1:	There, there, boss, don't cry.
Robber 2:	What's happened?
Big Bad Boss:	Someone has broken into our home. They've broken our photos.
Robber 1:	*(Looking really sad)* That's terrible, boss.
Big Bad Boss:	They've even stolen Fluffy.
Grandma:	Who's Fluffy?
Big Bad Boss:	He's my teddy bear. I've had him ever since I was a baby and now he's been stolen. *(Starts to suck his thumb and sob)*
Robber 2:	*(Almost crying)* Why do people do things like that?
Big Bad Boss:	Fluffy isn't worth much, but he means the world to me.
Wendy:	Ha! I don't believe I'm hearing this.
Rick:	Yeah! Serves you right! You treat people like this all the time.
Grandma:	Rick! Wendy! Leave him alone. Now is not the time—he's upset. Now he knows how people feel. *(To Big Bad Boss)* Would you like me to phone the police to report the burglary?
Big Bad Boss:	Would you? That's very kind. Maybe they can find Fluffy for me.
Grandma:	*(On her mobile phone)* Hello, PC BobUpAndDown. We are with the

Reproduced with permission from *The Cops & Robbers Holiday Club* by John Hardwick, published by Barnabas for Children 2014: www.barnabasinchurches.org.uk

Big Bad Boss. He wants to report a burglary. We're at the end of Letsby Avenue. You'll come straight away? I thought you might.

PC BobUpAndDown comes on stage and escorts the Big Bad Boss and the two robbers (who are all crying) off stage.

Grandma:	That's a bit of a sad ending.
Rick:	It's a brilliant ending. He got what he deserved.
Wendy:	No, I agree with Grandma. I don't like to see anyone upset like that, even if I think they deserve it.
Grandma:	Let's hope he'll learn from it and won't hurt other people again.
Narrator:	Wow! I wasn't expecting that. But hip, hip, hurray, the Watt family save the day again! Let's give three cheers for the Watt family and all the rest of the cast.

Play the Watt family theme tune.

Cops & Robbers crafts

Day 1: Policeman's cap

You will need:
Templates for a policeman's cap (see page 80); plastic or cardboard visor; sheet of blue craft foam; strip of black craft foam; small piece of yellow craft foam; stapler; glue

Staple the template pieces to the craft foam and cut out the shapes—a blue cap, black band and yellow badge. Glue the band and badge to the blue cap. Glue the cap to the visor.

Day 2: Decorate a purse

You will need:
Plain fabric purses (available from the internet); sticky felt letters and shapes

Joseph was sold into slavery and his brothers pocketed the money. Decorate fabric purses in any way you wish.

Day 3: Finger puppets

You will need:
Templates of a policeman and a robber (see page 81), photocopied on to thin card; scissors; colouring materials

Joseph was falsely accused and thrown in prison. Colour in and cut out the policeman and the robber. Cut out holes for fingers to go through, to make the legs of the characters.

Day 4: Pop-up puppet

You will need:
Templates for a paper cone and Joseph figure (see page 82); straws; glue; scissors; colouring pens. (Alternatively, pop-up puppet kits are available online: see, for example, www.bakerross.co.uk.)

Copy the cone template on to paper or thin card and decorate with bars to look like a prison. Draw Joseph on to the figure template and attach him to a straw as shown below. Joseph can now pop up from his prison.

Day 5: Making a mask

You will need:
Mask template (see page 83), photocopied on to thin card; pens; sticky felt; feathers; sequins

Joseph's brothers didn't recognise him because he looked and acted like an Egyptian. Decorate your mask in any way you wish, to make yourself look completely different from usual.

Cops & Robbers games

Stop in the name of the law!

Use a large but well-defined area in your venue, such as the hall. To play, you need two different 'bases', a suitable distance away from each other. They can be specific areas or objects that you need to touch, such as two walls. One of the bases is for the robbers and the other is the prison. When the robbers are at their base, they are safe and cannot be caught by the police.

Divide the children into two teams—cops and robbers. When the music plays (or a whistle or siren is blown once), the robbers leave their hide-out and the cops leave the prison. Both cops and robbers dance or walk around. When the music stops (or the whistle/siren is blown twice), the robbers dash back to their hide-out, chased by the police.

The cops have to catch all the robbers and lead them to the prison. To catch a robber, the cop must put both hands on the robber's shoulders. If they manage this, the robber must 'stop in the name of the law' and go with the cop to the prison. The cop can then go and catch more robbers.

Once they are caught, the robbers can't leave the prison unless another robber runs from their base to the prison and releases the imprisoned robber by touching his or her hand. They can then run back to their base and safety.

If the robbers are just sitting in their base and not coming out, the police are allowed to make the base 'unsafe' until some people leave. It ruins the game if no one runs out!

The winner of the game is the last robber to be caught.

Sleeping police officer

You will need:
A police hat or helmet; a blindfold

Sit the children in a circle with a chair in the middle. Choose a leader or a child to come and sit on the chair and put on the helmet.

Say that the police officer is very tired because of having to catch so many robbers and has put on a blindfold in order to nod off to sleep without anyone noticing. One by one, the children must try to sneak up and steal the police officer's helmet. If a child manages to steal the helmet and get back to their place before the cop wakes up, takes off their blindfold and catches them, then the new child becomes the sleeping police officer. But if the cop wakes up, removes their blindfold and manages to catch the child before they get back to their place, the same police officer nods off to sleep again.

Robbing the bank

You will need:
A small paddling pool or large container full of light, small play balls (or fake paper money); a police officer

Place the paddling pool in the middle of the playing area and fill it with either balls or paper money. Put a number (£1, £2, £5 or £10) on each of the play balls or fake paper notes.

Sit three or four teams, of equal numbers, in lines at different sides of the paddling pool and number the children in each team. Tell them that the paddling pool is a bank and that each ball or note is worth some money. There is only one police officer there to protect the bank.

When their number is called, each child with that number tries to dodge the police officer, grab a ball and take it back to their team. There will be three or four children—one from each team—running at the same time, making it very difficult for the police officer to catch them all.

(Please be fair and don't always go after the children from the same team, and be careful not to be too rough when running with the children.) If the police officer catches a child with a ball, the child has to put the ball back in the bank and return to their team with no money.

Once each child has had a turn, count up the money they have taken. The team with the most money is the winner.

Search for a clue

This is a treasure-hunt style game. Split the children into small groups of around five each and tell them that they are now clever detectives. Hide lots of small folded pieces of paper, showing different pictures, around the room or playing area. One set of papers should show pictures of get-away vehicles (sports car, tractor, taxi, beat-up old car, and so on). Another set should show different stolen objects (television, computer, piggy bank, jewellery box and so on—but not cars). The final set should show pictures of the criminal gang (these could be characters from Cluedo or holiday club team leaders).

Mark a value on the inside of each folded piece of paper. For example:

- A picture of a get-away vehicle is worth 5 points.
- A picture of a stolen object is worth 10 points.
- A picture of a member of the criminal gang is worth 20 points.

Each piece of paper is important, however large or small its value: it all goes toward the team's total amount.

Hide a gold star in one of the folded get-away vehicle papers, one of the stolen object papers, and one of the criminal gang papers. A paper with a gold star is worth double points.

The different groups of detectives are sent to find the folded pieces of paper, all at the same time. Once the time is up, each group of detectives counts up how many pieces of paper they have found.

The detective team with the most points is the winner.

Robber, Robber, Copper

(Play like 'Duck, Duck, Goose'.) Sit the children in a circle facing inwards. One child walks around the circle, touching each of the players on the head and saying 'robber'. If they say 'copper' instead, they run off and the person who has been touched gets up and chases them right round the circle.

If the robber gets back to the copper's place without being caught, the robber sits down and the new child takes a turn at walking round the circle. However, if the copper catches up with the robber, the copper sits down in their original place and the robber walks round the circle again.

Robbers and Coppers

This game works well if the children sit on chairs, but also works without chairs.

Sit the children in a circle facing inwards and with a gap between every three children. Choose two of the children. One is the copper, who stands in the centre of the circle. The other is the robber, who stands outside the circle.

When you say 'Go', the robber runs around the outside edge of the circle, trying to dodge the copper, who can chase in and out of the circle. The copper has ten seconds to catch the robber. The rest of the children count down slowly: '10, 9, 8, 7, 6, 5, 4, 3, 2, 1…'

If the copper catches the robber, the copper sits in the robber's place and the robber takes the copper's place in the centre of the circle. Choose another child to be the new robber and start the game again.

'Please, Mr Policeman'

This is a simple road safety game for younger children. You need one police officer or lollipop person and one speeding car driver.

The children stand at one side of the room. The idea is to get across to the other side safely. The police officer wants to get everyone across safely, so the children have to listen to his or her instructions carefully.

Explain to the children that the open space is a busy road. Say, 'Remember, never cross the road without looking left and right first, or while chatting to people or listening to your iPod or talking on your mobile phone. When it is safe to cross, walk straight across the road.' Repeat these words, quizzing the children as you go, to make sure they understand.

The children call to the policeman, 'Please, Mr Policeman, can we cross the road?' The policeman responds by saying, 'Only if it's safe to cross and you are wearing [colour].' Those who are wearing the right colour walk across the road safely, watched by the policeman.

The policeman then holds up a hand in the 'Halt!' position and says to the others: 'Please be careful and stay where you are! I can hear a speeding car!' The person pretending to drive a speeding car then goes past quickly.

Once again, the children who have not yet crossed the busy road call to the policeman, 'Please, Mr Policeman, can we cross the road?' The policeman responds by saying, 'Only if you are not chatting and it's safe to cross and have [a feature such as blue eyes or short hair].' The policeman holds up a hand to the remaining children, repeats the rhyme, and the speeding car goes past.

Repeat until all the children have safely crossed the road. Each time, the policeman adds another condition ('Only if you are… not listening to your iPod…' and so on.)

When the game has finished, say, 'We want everyone to cross safely and be a winner, because roads are too dangerous for games! Remember, never cross the road without looking left and right first, or while chatting to people or listening to your iPod or talking on your mobile phone. When it is safe to cross, walk straight across the road.'

Stuck in the jail

Choose two children, who chase the others like cops chasing robbers. Once a child is caught, they stand with their feet apart. Another child can set them free by crawling between their feet.

It's very tiring being the cops, so only keep this game going for a couple of minutes at a time before choosing different people to be the cops.

Puppet sketches

Day 1: The plot

Bert:	Hi, everyone! I think Lucy, my friend who talks almost as much as Wendy Watt, has just arrived. Here she comes.
Lucy:	*(Comes up)* I heard that! I don't talk anywhere near as much as Wendy Watt unless I'm in a bad mood.
Bert:	Well, you're not in a bad mood, are you?
Lucy:	Yes.
Bert:	You can't be. It's the first day of Cops & Robbers holiday club.
Lucy:	*(Looks up happily and jigs with delight)* Oh yes, I'm happy it's holiday club. I've been looking forward to it for ages.
Bert:	Good!
Lucy:	But I'm in a bad mood because…
Bert:	*(Bravely interrupting)* Oh no, what's wrong now?
Lucy:	It's my little brother. He's committed a terrible crime and been really mean… but I've plotted my revenge.
Bert:	I don't like the sound of that. What are you planning to do?
Lucy:	I'm plotting to peg him by his ears to the washing line.
Bert:	Ouch! That will hurt. He must have done something really mean to deserve something like that.
Lucy:	He has. Oh, I just thought—the washing line might break if I peg him to it. What else could I do? I know! I could paint his bicycle pink. He'll hate that.
Bert:	He certainly will. He loves his cool silver bicycle. Gosh, what has he done to deserve that?
Lucy:	I don't think we have any pink paint. I know, I could kidnap his teddy bear.

Bert:	No, Lucy, that's just going too far. What has he done to deserve you plotting against him in this way?
Lucy:	As I said, he's committed an unforgivable crime.
Bert:	Yes, but what?
Lucy:	My little brother Timmy has only gone and lent his Beano comic out to his best friend before I had a chance to read it.
Bert:	What? Is that all? Are you jealous?
Lucy:	What? Jealous that mum buys him the Beano comic and not me? Of course I… am!
Bert:	You do know, Lucy, that your brother uses his pocket money to buy the Beano, don't you?
Lucy:	*(Looks shocked)* No! I thought Mum bought him a present and not me, so…
Bert:	You became jealous—before you knew all the facts. Your little brother Timmy is a great guy, and normally you say he's the coolest little brother ever… and yet you want to punish him for a crime he hasn't committed!
Lucy:	Yeah, you're right. I'd better put his teddy back before he notices it's gone.
Bert:	And buy your own Beano.
Lucy:	Yes, I'll buy my own.
Both:	Bye, everyone, bye!

Reproduced with permission from *The Cops & Robbers Holiday Club* by John Hardwick, published by Barnabas for Children 2014: www.barnabasinchurches.org.uk

Day 2: The crime

Lucy: I had a plot to get out of the washing-up, but it didn't work. *(Bert's not listening as Lucy gabbles on)* Mum told me I had to wash up because I broke the dishwasher, so I thought, if I do a really bad job, then she won't want me to do it again. But instead she said, 'Lucy, you obviously need more practice!' and so I have to do it all week. Crime doesn't pay! *(Getting cross as she realises Bert isn't listening)* Are you listening to me?

Bert: No! Now leave me alone, Lucy. I've got my own problems.

Lucy: *(A bit shocked)* Oh, OK. It's not like you to snap at me. What's up?

Bert: Er… I don't want to talk about it.

Lucy: OK.

Bert: But then again, they say confession is good.

Lucy: What?

Bert: I've done something bad and I don't know what to do—whether to keep quiet and hope nobody notices, or lie about it, or tell the truth.

Lucy: Gosh, what have you done?

Bert: You know I've got a pet guinea pig called Chewing Gum?

Lucy: Yeah, she's so cute.

Bert: Yes, well, she did something terrible yesterday.

Lucy: What did she do?

Bert: She pooped and weed on and chewed my sister's picture, and ruined it.

Lucy: Oh no, that's terrible. I saw your sister's picture—she'd coloured it in so beautifully. She's very neat and tidy.

Bert: I know. Everyone kept going on about how beautiful and neat and tidy it was, and how her colouring was perfectly between the lines. 'A masterpiece,' Dad said. I'd done a picture too, but no one mentioned mine.

Lucy: Yes, but Bert—you always rush your colouring and you never bother about staying between the lines. It's a terrible shame! Your sister must be very upset.

Bert: She doesn't know yet. In fact, no one knows. I don't know how to tell them or what to say.

Lucy: Tell them the truth!

Bert: Yeah, but then I'll end up in big trouble.

Lucy: Why? It's not your fault if Chewing Gum got out of her cage and pooped, weed on and chewed your sister's picture, is it?

Bert: Who said Chewing Gum got out of her cage?

Lucy: How else would she get hold of it—unless someone posted it through the bars… and who would do such a mean thing? *(Looks at Bert, shocked)* Oh, Bert, please don't tell me that you posted your sister's masterpiece of a picture through the bars into Chewing Gum's cage.

Bert: OK, I won't.

Lucy: Good. *(Looks relieved)*

Bert: But I did.

Lucy: What? Oh, Bert, how could you?

Bert: I just became so jealous, with everyone going on about how brilliant her picture was and no one mentioning mine. When no one was looking, I took it and pushed it through the bars of the cage, and it didn't take Chewing Gum long to do her stuff. Now I feel terrible. How could I have done such a mean thing to my sister? What am I going to do?

Lucy: *(In a harsh voice)* As I said, tell the truth.

Bert: Yes, but…

Lucy: Be a man and own up to your crime.

Bert: Yes, but I'll get into big trouble.

Lucy: Yes, probably, but I'm sure they will forgive you in time. But if you lie, then you'll have to lie again and again until, in the end, no one will be able to trust you—including me.

Bert: You're right. I'd better go and confess and say a huge 'sorry'—and try to think of a way I can make up for being such a mean big brother.

Both: Bye, everyone!

Lucy: Hey Bert, are you still soggy?

Bert: No, but is your dad's car still soggy?

Lucy: Oh, I'd better explain to this lot what we're going on about. When my dad got home from work yesterday, he said that his car was in a right mess.

Bert: He'd parked under a tree and the birds had obviously been using his car for target practice. It was in a right yucky state.

Lucy: Then he said something amazing—he's never said anything like it before. He said…

Bert: 'How would you like to earn some money and clean my car for me?'

Lucy: 'Yes, please,' we said, and we got to work straight away with buckets of soapy water.

Bert: Hosepipe at the ready.

Lucy: After about ten minutes, Dad came out and wasn't impressed because we were soaked but the car was still dry.

Bert: Yeah, but it was a great water fight. Then we started to clean the car, and, even if I do say so myself, we are very good car cleaners.

Lucy: The hardest bit was cleaning the roof because we couldn't reach.

Bert: But we soon worked out how to squirt water from the hose up in the air so that it came down on the roof.

Lucy: That's when it all went horribly wrong. Dad suddenly came dashing out and shouted 'STOP!' He was just about to shout something else when…

Bert: I turned to see what was up…

Lucy: … and squirted the hose right in his mouth. He had a mouth full of water and it knocked him over.

Bert: Oopsy!

Lucy: Yes, oopsy indeed!

Bert: He was soaked through, so I quickly turned the hose away from him so that the water was coming down on the roof of the car again.

Lucy: Dad stood up and again shouted 'STOP!' at the top of his voice.

Bert: And you'll never guess what happened next. I turned and accidentally squirted water at him again, but this time he managed to dodge it…

Lucy: … by stepping out of the way—but he stepped right into my bucket of dirty, cold water.

Bert: He didn't seem to notice. He was too busy shouting at me—something about the sun roof being open. I turned and looked though the window of the car and there was a lake.

Lucy: Yeah, inside Dad's car, and the water was still coming in. I tried to crack a joke and said, 'Let's go fishing,' but Dad didn't find it funny. In fact, he was really cross.

Bert: He even shouted at me. Then he dashed across and opened the car door.

Lucy: It was like Niagara Falls. The water gushed out…

Bert: … knocking your dad over again.

Lucy: What happened next was very funny. It was like slow motion. The bucket flew off his foot…

Bert: … through the air…

Lucy: … and landed on his head.

Bert: A soggy dad with a bucket of water on his head!

Lucy: Good job the bucket was on his head because Dad was still shouting, and I don't think it was anything very pleasant.

Bert: That's when I remembered I had to be somewhere else, quickly.

Lucy: Yes, you ran off and left me. I switched off the hose… Dad took the bucket off his head… I half smiled at him, but he didn't smile back. He didn't say a word, and he went back in the house, taking the bucket with him.

Bert: So is now a good time to ask for my money?

Lucy: What money?

Bert: My money for cleaning your dad's car.

Lucy: *(Angry) What?* It was your entire fault! It was you spraying the water in the car, you squirted my dad with water, and you ran off and left me.

Bert: Hey, that's not fair, Lucy! I didn't know the sun roof was open on your dad's car, and I didn't squirt him in the mouth with water on purpose, and I had to dash off because I suddenly realised I was late for my tea.

Lucy: I'm sorry if I've falsely accused you, Bert, but Dad told me off again this

Reproduced with permission from *The Cops & Robbers Holiday Club* by John Hardwick, published by Barnabas for Children 2014: www.barnabasinchurches.org.uk

morning. He's really upset, because he loves his car and it's still wet.

Bert: That's not fair! It's not your fault, either.

Lucy: That's exactly what Dad said next. He said, 'Sorry, Lucy, that wasn't fair. It wasn't your fault, it was mine, for leaving the sun roof open.' I gave him a big hug because I could see he needed it.

Bert: We'd better go—but *(To audience)* if anyone needs their car washing, we're the people to see!

Both: Bye!

Bert comes out with a bandage round his arm.

Lucy: Ouch! That looks painful. What have you done, Bert?

Bert: I've hurt my arm.

Lucy: Oh, I thought you'd hurt your leg.

Bert: Really?

Lucy: No, you big banana! It's obvious you've hurt your arm, but how?

Bert: I went up the park with some friends to play football. Some guys came along and challenged us to a match.

Lucy: So you did this playing football?

Bert: Sort of... The other guys said that we would play without any rules. Everyone could do as they liked.

Lucy: What? You can't play football without any rules.

Bert: We know that now, but at the time it sounded like a great idea. No rules, do as you like, no one to tell you what you can and can't do. No one blowing the whistle and stopping the game all the time.

Lucy: Oh dear! What happened?

Bert: One minute they had eleven goalies...

Lucy: Eleven goalies? You can't have eleven goalies.

Bert: You can when there are no rules. Then they ran off with the goalposts.

Lucy: Cor! They must be strong!

Bert: We'd used our coats as posts. Then they picked up the ball when they weren't meant to—but they were allowed to because there weren't any rules.

Lucy: Oh dear. It doesn't sound like much fun to me.

Bert: The one time I had the ball, I dribbled it past the first player, and the next, and another one. Then suddenly they all jumped on me and picked up the ball and ran off with it. That's when I hurt my arm.

Lucy: So was it a good game?

Bert: No! It was stupid! It wasn't a game at all. It was a riot and they stole the ball.

Lucy: Oh dear!

Bert: Then Mum was cross with me when I told her I'd lost my new football. She said I'd been foolish trying to play football without rules.

Lucy: Yes, she's right.

Bert:	Oh, don't you start! It was a horrible day. I lost my ball, hurt my arm and got into trouble with Mum all at the same time. I'm never going to play football again.
Lucy:	But you love football. Don't let those silly people put you off doing something you enjoy! Just make sure everyone knows what the rules are, next time.
Bert:	Good idea!
Lucy:	Hey, Bert, let's have a game of footie without any rules.
Bert:	Watch it! *(Chasing her off stage)*
Both:	Bye, everyone!

Day 5: Forgiveness isn't easy

Bert:	*(To audience)* Lucy was going to the circus last night with her mates. I wonder how she got on. *(Lucy comes up)* So, Lucy, was it good?
Lucy:	What?
Bert:	The circus.
Lucy:	Oh, the circus. Yes, apparently, apparently, yes.
Bert:	Excellent! Were there clowns?
Lucy:	Apparently, yes.
Bert:	Flying trapeze?
Lucy:	Apparently, yes.
Bert:	Tightrope walkers?
Lucy:	Apparently, yes.
Bert:	A candy floss store?
Lucy:	Apparently, yes.
Bert:	So it was great?
Lucy:	Oh. Apparently, yes, yes, yes, apparently, apparently, yes.
Bert:	Lucy, why do you keep saying 'apparently'?
Lucy:	Huh! Why do I keep saying 'apparently'? I'll tell you why. Because my so-called best mates were meant to pick me up, but they forgot me.
Bert:	Oh, no! So you didn't go! Wait a minute. Then how do you know it was such a great time?
Lucy:	Because right at the very end they remembered me and came round to apologise, and told me what a great time they'd had.
Bert:	Oh, Lucy! Maybe you can go another night.
Lucy:	No… *(Very sad)* it was the circus's last performance in our town. I've missed out. But don't worry, I've planned how I will get my own back.
Bert:	I don't like the sound of that. What are you planning to do?
Lucy:	I'm having a mega party. There will be clowns, flying trapeze, tightrope walkers, a candy floss store, and everyone is invited.
Bert:	Great!
Lucy:	Apart from those so-called friends of mine.
Bert:	Hang on, Lucy! We all need friends, but friends are bound to let us down from time to time. If you're not careful, you'll have no friends to climb trees with… *(To audience)* Lucy is a bit of a tomboy… *(Back to Lucy)* or play football with, or

	lots of things. If you invite them, they'll be so surprised, and they'll know that you are a really great friend.
Lucy:	I know you're right, but it's so hard. They left me out.
Bert:	Forgiving is always hard, but we need to remember, we all let people down. How would you feel if someone refused to forgive you?
Lucy:	You're right. OK. I'll invite them. Now excuse me, I have a party to organise.
Both:	Bye, everyone!

Bible story dramatised narrations

- In order to bring the narration to life, make sure that you have practised beforehand. This applies even when reading the story from a script.
- Experiment with several different voices and try to vary the tone and level of your voice—for example, using a whisper, speaking loudly in some places and softly in others, and using expressions to denote sadness, happiness and so on.
- Add simple movement or hand gestures to match words, such as looking at the audience, turning away, waving a finger and so on.
- Practise with other members of the cast to synchronise some of the movements, to mime some of the story as it is narrated, or to speak some lines in unison to emphasise certain words.
- Try performing the script as a monologue or adding music, sound effects and movement.

These Bible story narrations are available from www.johnhardwick.org.uk.

Day 1: The plot

Don't be jealous!

* Bible story: Genesis 37:1–11

> **Key points**
> * Spoilt Joseph shows off his new cool coat, and his brothers are jealous. Spoilt Joseph shares his dreams, in which he is the main man and others worship him. His brothers are furious and start to plot against him.
> * Although his brothers plotted bad things for Joseph, God planned good things for him— but he had some important lessons to learn along the way.
> * It's good to try to understand what caused the problem in the first place: (1) a father who had a favourite out of his twelve sons; (2) a spoilt son who may have believed he was better than the rest; (3) a family of brothers whose jealousy turned into bitterness and caused them to hatch a wicked plot.
>
> **Cast**
> * Narrator and two others (A and B)

Narrator:	We want to tell you a story about a family.
A:	A large family.
B:	In fact, a very, very large family.
Narrator:	Just imagine that [A and B: insert their names] were brothers [sisters/ brother and sister], and one day [A] said to [B]…
A:	*(In a posh voice)* Look at my huge bar of chocolate from Mummy and Daddy!
B:	Why did you get that?
A:	I got 10 out of 10 in my spelling test. Would you like some chocolate?
B:	Yes, please!
A:	Then get 10 out of 10 in your spellings and get your own. But we all know that won't happen, 'cos you're not clever like me! *(Pops chocolate in mouth and speaks with a full mouth)* You're not jealous, are you? Tut, tut, jealousy is a terrible thing!
B:	So is eating with your mouth full and showing off.
Narrator:	*(To audience)* If that happened to you, I bet you'd be jealous. Well, that's exactly what happened in today's

Bible story. Dad, whose name was Jacob, also known as Israel, had twelve sons. One day he splashed out loads of money on…

A:	*(Interrupts excitedly)* I know this story! He splashed out on new coats for all his sons.
Narrator:	Er, not quite. He splashed out loads of money on an amazing, fantastic, exciting, incredible and colourful coat…
A:	For his wife?
Narrator:	No.
A:	For himself?
Narrator:	No.
A:	For whom, then?
Narrator:	Joseph.
B:	Hey, can I play the part of the spoilt son Joseph with his posh coat?
Narrator:	I suppose so.

Give B a smart coat or jacket to put on.

B:	*(Excited)* I love it! *(Walking across stage like a model on a catwalk)* I feel like a [king/queen] in this. Can I have a crown, too?
A:	*(Jealous)* Who does [he/she] think [he/she] is? It's such an uncool coat— definitely last season, darling!
B:	You're so jealous, aren't you?
A:	Oh no, I'm not.
B:	Oh yes, you are.
A:	Well, maybe I am. But I'm sure Dad will buy me an even more amazing coat next.

Narrator shakes head, looking sad, and B shakes head, looking smug and happy.

Narrator:	No, I'm afraid Dad bought the amazing coat for Joseph, but he didn't buy one for the rest of his sons. Joseph's brothers were hurt that their dad seemed to love Joseph more than the rest of them, and they became very jealous of Joseph. But sadly, Joseph made it worse. Just imagine if your brother or sister said to you…
A:	*(To narrator)* Last night I had a dream.
Narrator:	Oh, really?
A:	Yes, I dreamt that our [latest fashionable toy] came to life and your [latest toys] bowed down to my [latest toy] and made him their king.

Reproduced with permission from *The Cops & Robbers Holiday Club* by John Hardwick, published by Barnabas for Children 2014: www.barnabasinchurches.org.uk

Narrator:	Oh, really? So are you saying that your [latest toy] is better than my [latest toy]?
A:	No.
Narrator:	Good!
A:	I was simply saying that the dream must mean I'm better than you and you are going to make me your king.
Narrator:	In your dreams, mate! Now back to the Bible story. That's exactly what Joseph said to his brothers—apart from the fact that it wasn't a [latest toy]…
B:	*(Still wearing the coat, very smug)* Brothers, in your rather old and scruffy coats, listen to this!
A:	*(Rough voice)* What do you want?
B:	*(Smug voice)* Last night I had a dream. We were all binding sheaves of corn out in the field when suddenly mine rose and stood up. Then all your sheaves of corn gathered round mine—and, guess what they did. Go on, guess what they did!
A:	No idea.
B:	Bowed down to it! Your corn bowed down to my corn. How cool is that?
A:	*(Angry)* Let me at him!
Narrator:	Calm down, [name of A].
A:	Who does he think he is? Does he think that we will all bow down to him? Does he think that he will rule over us?
Narrator:	Then Joseph said…
B:	*(Smug voice)* Hang on, I haven't finished yet. There's more.
A:	More?!
B:	Yes! I had another dream. This time the sun and the moon and eleven stars all started bowing down to me. It was so cool!
Narrator:	This time, even Joseph's dad, Jacob, became cross with him. 'Look, son, what is this dream you had? Will your mother and I and your brothers all bow down to you?'
B:	*(Shrugs shoulders, extremely smug, with a big smile)*
A:	No chance, mate! Who does he think he is?
Narrator:	Yes, sadly, Joseph's brothers became so angry with him that they started to plot against him. I'm sure his brothers were good lads, really, but their jealousy was turning into hatred and there was trouble ahead.
B:	*(Taking off his coat)* Let's not be like Joseph, thinking we're better than others.
A:	Let's not be like his brothers, being jealous of others.
Narrator:	None of Joseph's brothers even considered that maybe God had given Joseph those dreams or wondered what they might mean. God gives different gifts to different people, so let us try not to be jealous, but thank God for the gifts he gives each of us.

Reproduced with permission from *The Cops & Robbers Holiday Club* by John Hardwick, published by Barnabas for Children 2014: www.barnabasinchurches.org.uk

Day 2: The crime

Speak the truth!

• Bible story: Genesis 37:12–36

> **Key points**
> • Joseph's brothers seize an opportunity and Joseph is sold into slavery. But the crime does not pay, as they have to lie to their father and their lives are ruined by guilt.
> • Joseph is helpless and no one can help him but God.
>
> **Cast**
> • Narrator and two others (A and B)

Narrator: *(To A+B)* I have two parts in this story again. Who wants to play which part?

A+B: Tell us what the parts are.

Narrator: One is a gang of hardworking lads who go out to the fields to look after their sheep, protecting them against wild animals. The other part is a lazy, spoilt boy with cool clothes who doesn't seem to have to go to work with the rest of them.

A+B: *(Both with hands in the air, over-enthusiastic)* Please, please, can I be the lazy, spoilt boy with the cool clothes who doesn't go to work?

Narrator: Calm down, calm down! Look, to save any arguments, let's stick to the same roles as yesterday.

Narrator gives the cool coat to B, who instantly looks smug again.

A: Oh, that's not fair!

Narrator: Yep, that's exactly what Joe's brothers thought, because it seemed as if they had to go to work while Joe stayed at home having all the fun and being given gifts, like cool coats and stuff.

B: *(Very smug, turning to A)* Did you hear that? Off to work you go! Reminds me of a song. *(Sings and waves as A walks crossly off stage)* 'Hi ho, hi ho, it's off to work you go!' *(To Narrator)* They've gone! Jolly good show—it's so much better when it's just you and me, Daddy. Let's go play!

Narrator: *(Sternly)* I'm the Narrator, not your daddy! Anyway, as you know, your brothers are looking after the sheep in the fields, quite a distance away. I'm going to send you to them.

B: *(Shocked)* Who, me?

Narrator: Yes, you!

B: Oh, go on then—very well! *(Whispers to audience)* Maybe if I do as Daddy says, he'll give me another present.

Narrator: I'm not your daddy! Go on—off you go!

B: All right, I'm going, I'm going.

B walks off stage, dragging his feet. A comes on stage.

A: *(Pointing into the distance)* Don't wander off, Ba-a-a-a-bra! I must be going mad. Not only do I smell of sheep but I'm starting to sound like them, too. I wonder what Joe is doing now? He's probably still in bed, dreaming. I wonder what his dreams are about this time. I suppose I'll be bowing down to him again.

Narrator: He's not still in bed dreaming. He's on his way to see you.

A: Oh, spying for Dad, is he?

Narrator: As Joseph's brothers saw him in the distance, one of them said…

A: Oh look, here comes that dreamer. I know! *(Wicked voice, rubbing hands together)* Let's grab him and kill him and throw him down a well. Then hopefully a wild animal will come along and gobble him up for dinner.

Narrator: *(Sarcastically)* As you can tell, his brothers really loved him… not! When Reuben, Joseph's oldest brother, heard this, he was horrified. But he could see how angry the rest of the brothers were, so he quickly said, 'Don't kill him or shed his blood. Just put him in the well. We can decide what to do with him later.'

A: *(Crossly)* Spoilsport!

Narrator: Reuben planned to rescue Joseph later.

B: *(Wandering in)* Hi, chaps. Did you see me coming in my cool coat that you're all so jealous of?

A: Get him!

A grabs B and mimes beating him up, taking hold of one arm of the coat and spinning B round so that the coat comes off, then pushing him in the back. B mimes falling into the well, screaming.

A: Didn't we do well? Hey, do you get it? I said, 'Didn't we do *well*'? And we've pushed him in a *well*! Shame there's no water in it—oh well! Ha! I said it again! 'Oh well!'

Narrator: *(Disgusted)* It's not funny! Meanwhile, Joe landed in the well with a thump.

B: Ouch! That hurt. If you've ripped my coat, you're for it.

A: Oh, we're so scared.

B: *(Almost crying)* I'm going to tell Daddy on you.

Narrator: Reuben went off to think about how he could rescue Joseph, while the rest of the brothers sat down to eat. Isn't that incredible? They had just thrown their brother in a well but they didn't feel at all guilty. Instead, they sat down to enjoy a good meal! *(A mimes eating lunch)*

B: Can I have some food? I'm starving.

A: *(Aggressively)* No!

Narrator: Suddenly the brothers looked up from their meal and saw a caravan of Ishmaelites—very rich businessmen, riding grand camels, on their way to Egypt.

A: *(Stands up, mouth full of food)* I've had a great idea! If we sell Joseph as a slave to those rich men, then they'll take him all the way to Egypt—and that's a long, long way away. So we'll never see him again and we'll make loads of money all at the same time.

Narrator: That's a wicked plan!

A: I know. Ha, good, isn't it?

Narrator: And that's exactly what they did. *(A and B mime)* They pulled Joseph up out of the well.

B: *(Sobbing)* About time! I'm going to tell Daddy on you.

A: Shut up!

A gags B and marches him off stage.

Narrator: They sold their own flesh and blood, their own brother, for 20 pieces of silver. They watched as Joseph was tied up and led away to be sold as a slave in Egypt. Reuben didn't return in time, and failed to save him.

A: *(Runs back on stage, jumping for joy)* What a brilliant chap I am! We've got rid of that spoilt dreamer of a brother once and for all and made money all at the same time.

Narrator: And what are you going to tell your dad?

A: *(Face drops)* Oh. We... er... never thought of that.

Narrator: You could always tell him the truth—how you sold your own brother as a slave. Maybe you could mount a rescue. Maybe it's not too late!

A: Tell Dad we sold him as a slave? Do we look stupid?

Narrator: I won't answer that.

A: It's obvious! There are all kinds of wild animals round here. In fact, we have to work really hard protecting the sheep.

Narrator: *(Sarcastically)* You protect your sheep but sell your brother.

A: Where's his coat? We'll rip his coat, cover it with blood, pretend to find it out in the field and take it home to Dad.

Narrator: Tell a lie to your own dad?

A: No. We won't have to. Dad will recognise the coat and will assume Joseph has been killed by a wild animal. I amaze myself, I'm so clever! Now let's go and find some blood for the coat.

A goes off stage.

Narrator: That's exactly what they did—and their dad did recognise Joseph's coat straight away. He saw all the blood and how it was torn apart and he knew that his son Joseph was dead. It broke his heart. His brothers had never seen him so upset. Day after day, week after week, month after month, he wept for his son, and Joseph's brothers deeply regretted what they had done on that foolish day.

A: *(Comes on stage looking sad)* I wish we could go back in time. I wish we hadn't done that to Joseph. I wish we hadn't had to lie to Dad. I wish we hadn't broken his heart.

Narrator: But it was too late for them. Let's not make their mistake—let's not make a snap decision that we'll regret, and then have to lie to try to get out of it.

A: Lying just made things worse for us.

Narrator: Let's do our best to 'always tell the truth and refuse to tell a lie'.

Reproduced with permission from *The Cops & Robbers Holiday Club* by John Hardwick, published by Barnabas for Children 2014: www.barnabasinchurches.org.uk

Day 3: Falsely accused

Hold on tightly!

- Bible story: Genesis 39

Key points
- Just when everything seems to be going quite well for Joseph in Egypt and he is growing up and turning into a kind and thoughtful young man, he becomes the victim of another terrible crime. Potiphar's wife admires him and wants him as her lover—but Joseph does the right thing and refuses her.
- Angry that she can't get her own way, Potiphar's wife falsely accuses Joseph and he is sent to jail.

Cast
- Narrator and two others (A and B)

Narrator starts by singing and doing actions to 'Walk like an Egyptian'.

Narrator: If you remember, the spoilt son with the cool coat had a bad day. In fact, it was the most awful day. His own brothers sold him to some passing traders, who dragged him off to Egypt.

B: My dreams certainly didn't come true. Instead of my brothers bowing down to me, they sold me to be a slave. They must really hate me.

Narrator: I reckon Joe must have been wondering why. What had he done to deserve this? And eventually the penny dropped.

B: I've been acting like a spoilt brat, showing off with my new coat. I did have those dreams, but I used them to show off rather than trying to find out what God was saying through them.

Narrator: When Joseph arrived in Egypt, he would have been in a right state— hot and very, very tired. No cool coat now! No more showing off. But guess what the Bible says? Even though Joseph had lost everything and was a nobody, God was with him. God hadn't deserted him. Thank you, Bible, for reminding us that God is with us during the bad times too.

B: Yeah, I'm doing all right for a slave! I've been bought by one of the king of Egypt's important men, an official

to the Pharaoh. And Potiphar—don't laugh, it's not his fault he's called Potiphar—anyway, Potiphar, he's all right. He's a good guy.

Narrator: Joseph forgot all about the dreams in which he was the one in charge and everything bowed down to him.

B: Aw, that's just a dream!

Narrator: He faithfully served Potiphar, and Potiphar was so impressed with his new slave that he put Joseph in charge of the whole house. He became the top slave.

B: Yes, it's all going really well. Despite everything that happened to me before, I know that God is with me, helping me.

Narrator: Even Potiphar realised that God was helping Joseph.

B: Everything's going well, apart from…

Narrator: (*Interrupts*) What?

B: Potiphar's wife. She's got the hots for me.

Narrator: Pardon?

B: She fancies me.

Narrator: How do you know?

B: She's always following me around, blowing me kisses, stroking my hair… do I need to go on?

Narrator: Oh boy, what are you going to do?

B: What can I do? I respect my master, Potiphar. Anyway, she's not my type. I know I shouldn't be surprised, though. After all, I am well built and terribly handsome.

Narrator: Ha, in your dreams!

B: No, it says so in the Bible, so it must be true. Look in Genesis chapter 39 verse 6.

Narrator: Yes, it certainly does—and it also says that Potiphar's wife didn't give up.

A comes on stage, wearing a long wig.

A: Come here, gorgeous!

B panics and runs away.

A: Give me a kissy, kissy. I want you! (*Chases B off stage*)

Narrator: Thankfully, Joseph did get away, but Potiphar's wife grabbed his cloak while he was escaping. Then, when her husband Potiphar got home, she told wicked lies about Joseph, saying

Reproduced with permission from *The Cops & Robbers Holiday Club* by John Hardwick, published by Barnabas for Children 2014: www.barnabasinchurches.org.uk

that Joseph had tried to kiss her and wouldn't leave her alone. Potiphar was so furious that he had Joseph arrested and flung into the king's prison. Poor Joseph—and just when everything was going so well. But guess what awesome thing the Bible says: 'But while Joseph was in prison God was with him!' Joe was having a really hard time, but he still put his trust in God and was holding on tightly to him.

And the jail-break to freedom!

- Bible story: Genesis 40—41

Key points
- From bad to worse! Joseph hasn't done anything wrong. In fact, he chose to do what was right, yet he is still sent to jail. How unfair it must seem!
- But God hasn't forgotten him. He is still with Joseph during this difficult time, and turns Joseph's life right round as he gives him the answer to the Pharaoh's dreams.
- Joseph is set free, saves the nation and becomes the second most powerful man in Egypt.

Cast
- Narrator and two others (A and B)

Narrator:	Joseph was no longer a spoilt son with a cool coat, and he was no longer the head slave for Potiphar. He was now a slave flung into the king's jail for a crime he hadn't even committed. But he didn't sulk or moan at God.
B:	I thought people were going to bow down to me. I thought I was more important than everyone else, but I'm not. I'm just a nobody.
Narrator:	God rarely chooses big-headed people. He chooses people who know they need him—and God was with Joseph.
A:	(Roughly, to B) New prisoner, eh? Well, I'm the boss of this here prison, so if there's anything you want, don't hesitate to ask. You won't get it, mind! Right, Joe, get in that cell. You'll be sharing it with the king's ex-cupbearer and the king's ex-baker. (Big sigh) I suppose I'd better get back to the paperwork now. I have hundreds of horrible prisoners to sort out, too much to do and not enough hours in the day.
B:	I could help.
A:	You? But you're just a no-good slave prisoner.
B:	Yes, but I was in charge of Potiphar's household until his wife took a fancy to me.

A:	Ha, she fancies everyone. But you were in charge, eh? You must be a smart guy.
Narrator:	So that's what Joseph did. He didn't moan; instead he made himself useful and, before long, gained the respect of everyone in the prison.
A:	This place has never run so smoothly. I'm going to put you in charge of all the prisoners.
Narrator:	One night, Joseph's two cellmates both had dreams that made them sad.
B:	Why the glum face?
Narrator:	'I had a dream,' said the cupbearer, 'and I can't get it out of my mind. Can you tell me what it means?'
B:	No, not me—but God can. Tell me your dream.
Narrator:	'I dreamed about a grapevine that had three branches. As soon as it budded, it blossomed, and soon it was covered in clusters of juicy grapes. I squeezed the juice into the king's cup and served him the delicious and refreshing drink.'
B:	Sounds yummy! The three branches on the grapevine mean three days. In three days you will serve your king again. Hey, don't forget to mention me to the king, because I didn't do anything wrong and I shouldn't be in here.
Narrator:	'I also had a dream,' said the baker.
B:	Go on, then, tell me your dream.
Narrator:	'I was balancing three baskets of delicious cakes and bread for the king on my head. That's got to be good news, hasn't it? Is that three days too?'
B:	Was that the end of the dream?
Narrator:	'Er, no. Then some birds came along and ate the bread—cheeky things!'
B:	Three baskets does also mean three days.
Narrator:	'So I'll be set free in three days—cool!'
B:	Sorry, but there's more. Just as the birds lifted the bread out of the basket, the king is going to lift your head off.
Narrator:	(A big gulp) 'I'm going to lose my head?'
B:	I'm afraid so.
Narrator:	Joseph—or should I say, God—was spot on, and the cupbearer went back to serving the king again. But sadly he forgot all about Joseph until two years later…

B:	Two years? He left me in the cell for another two years? Thanks a lot!
Narrator:	… when Pharaoh had a dream. He said… (A interrupts)
A:	Can I play the part of the king? I've always wanted to be a king! (Puts a crown on his head)
Narrator:	Oh, go on, then. Now, back to the story. One night Pharaoh had a dream, and he said…
A:	(Big posh voice) I'm the king!
Narrator:	We know you're the king. Just get on with it!
A:	OK, then. (Posh king voice) In my dream I was standing by the River Nile when I saw seven fat cows. Then suddenly seven ugly skinny cows came out of the River Nile and gobbled up the seven fat cows.
Narrator:	(Laughs)
A:	It wasn't funny—it was scary.
Narrator:	(Stops laughing, nods sincerely) Yes, very scary.
A:	The dream is so clear in my mind, it must mean something. But that wasn't the end of it. I had another dream.
Narrator:	Another one?
A:	(Snaps) Yes, why? Am I boring you?
Narrator:	Oh, no, Sire!
A:	Good! In the next dream I saw seven ears of good-looking healthy corn all on one stalk and…
Narrator:	(Interrupting) Can corn be good-looking?
A:	What? Oh, don't interrupt. I'm the king, you know! Then seven thin ears of corn, that had been scorched by the heat of the sun, gobbled up the healthy ones, and that was the end of my dreams. They are so clear in my mind that they must mean something. (Claps hands to summon wise men) Wise men, tell me what these dreams mean!
Narrator:	But none of the king's wise men had any idea. Then suddenly the king's cupbearer remembered Joseph…
B:	About time!
Narrator:	… and told Pharaoh all about how Joseph had told him and the baker the meaning of their dreams, and how they had come true.
A:	(Posh king voice) Fetch him! I say, fetch him immediately!

Narrator:	Wow! Can you imagine? Suddenly Joseph was taken out of his cell and was standing in front of the most powerful man in the world.
A:	My cupbearer reckons you're a very wise man because you interpreted his dream. Is this correct?
B:	No.
A:	*(Shocked)* What do you mean, no? Can you or can't you tell me what my dream means?
B:	No.
A:	No?
B:	I can't, but I know a God who can.
Narrator:	Did you hear that? Joseph didn't take the credit for himself but talked about his God with the king of the land. He gave God the credit.
A:	I can see you are very smart—because if it turns out that you can't tell me my dream, it's not your fault but your God's, I suppose.
B:	Oh, nothing like that! I know God can tell you your dream.
A:	OK, well, seven thin cows ate seven fat cows, and seven thin ears of corn ate seven fat ears of corn.
B:	Oh, that's easy!
A:	*(Shocked)* Is it?
B:	Yes, the seven fat cows and the good ears of corn are basically the same dream. They mean seven good years— good crops, plenty for everyone and a good time.
A:	Sounds exciting!
B:	But then the seven thin cows that ate the fat cows, and the bad ears of corn that ate the good corn mean that there will be a terrible famine. There will be no crops and no food. The land will be dry for seven long years.
A:	Sounds terrible! What can we do?
B:	Could I make a suggestion?
A:	Please do!
B:	I suggest that you choose a wise person to be put in charge of all of Egypt. That person should have huge new cities built—cities to store food. During the seven years of good harvests, they should collect a fifth of the harvest and store it all in the food cities. Then, when the seven years of famine come, you will have food for your people and it can be distributed fairly.
A:	So I need a wise person, eh? I know the perfect man for the job!
B+Narrator:	Who?
A:	*(Pointing at B)* You!
B:	*(Amazed)* Me?
A:	It's very obvious that you are wise, and, even better, you have God on your side. The God who can interpret dreams is a very wise God indeed and it's wonderful to know that he will be guiding you during this difficult time. You will be put in charge of the whole of Egypt, and there will be none greater than you. Apart from me, of course—I'm still the king!
Narrator:	Fantastic! Did you hear that? Joseph was a slave prisoner just this morning and now he has become the second most powerful person in Egypt. Isn't God amazing? If God can do that with Joseph, I wonder what God has planned for you!

Reproduced with permission from *The Cops & Robbers Holiday Club* by John Hardwick, published by Barnabas for Children 2014: www.barnabasinchurches.org.uk

Day 5: Forgiveness isn't easy

Hard choices

- Bible story: Genesis 42—45

Key points
- To Joseph's astonishment, his brothers kneel before him, asking for food. Joseph's appearance has changed so much that the brothers don't realise it is Joseph—fulfilling Joseph's earlier dream in which they bowed before him.
- Can Joseph really forgive the ones who have hurt him and tried to destroy his life? He sets them some tests to see if they have changed.

Cast
- Narrator and two others (A and B)

Narrator:	What an amazing story! If you remember, yesterday Joseph went from being a slave in prison to the second most powerful man in all of Egypt in just one day. He has come a long way from being the selfish, spoilt son of Jacob. He even looks like an Egyptian now. Even his own family wouldn't recognise him any more!
B:	Pharaoh had a dream and God told me what it meant. There would be seven years of plenty, which meant plenty of food, which meant plenty of happy people. We stored a fifth of the grain in our food cities, just as God had guided me to do, and, oh boy, it's a good job we did because now we've entered into the seven years of famine.
Narrator:	It's bad, very bad! In other countries where they didn't store their grain, people are starving.
B:	In Egypt we have some rumbling tummies from time to time, but we have enough grain to last the seven years. It's my job to make sure we use just the right amount each year. I can't afford to run out.
Narrator:	Yes, Joseph was a very powerful and respected man. People in other lands were desperate and would travel miles to buy grain from Egypt. They would fall at Joseph's feet and beg him to sell them grain.
B:	(Shocked) No! Surely this can't be happening!
Narrator:	What?
B:	They're here, bowing before me, begging to buy some food.
Narrator:	Who?
B:	Ten of them! From Canaan!
Narrator:	Hey, that's where you're from. Do you know them?
B:	Of course I do! I recognised them straight away, but they don't recognise me.
Narrator:	I bet that's nice, meeting people you used to know.
B:	I haven't told them who I am. In fact, I was very rude to them.
Narrator:	Rude, you? That's not like you—well, not any more. You used to be rude and selfish when you were a spoilt little boy, but God has changed you.
B:	Has he?
Narrator:	Now if your brothers had the cheek to turn up begging for food, I could understand you being rude to them, but that's not likely to hap… (Realises what he has said)
B:	(Nodding) Yep, it's them, ten of my brothers, bowing down to me just like in my dreams all those years ago.
A:	(Enters, bowing head to B) Please, my Lord, we are ten brothers from Canaan. We've come to buy food.
B:	(Snaps) You're spies!
A:	(Shocked) Spies? Do I look like a spy?
Narrator:	If you looked like a spy, then you wouldn't be a very good one.
A:	(To Narrator) Keep out of this, you! (To B) No, my Lord, we are not spies but honest men, throwing ourselves on your mercy. We are here to buy food, that's all.
B:	(Aggressively) No. You have come to see where Egypt is unprotected so that you can attack us.
A:	No, my Lord, we're just twelve brothers from Canaan.
B:	Er, hello? There are only ten of you.
A:	Oh yeah. Well, our youngest brother stayed at home with Dad and our other brother is no more.
Narrator:	I bet I can guess what happened to him!
A:	(Confused) What?
B:	Prove it!

A:	What do you mean?
B:	Nine of you can go home and fetch your younger brother. Guard, throw that one *(Pointing to A)* in jail! They'll all have to come back if they want to see him again.
Narrator:	Joseph…
A:	I had a brother called Joseph!
Narrator:	*(To A)* Please don't interrupt! Joseph gave the brothers some grain and told them to take it to their starving family, saying that they must return with their younger brother to prove they were telling the truth.
B:	*(Almost sobbing)* Oh, I can't handle this!
A:	What is going on?
B:	I can sort out the grain for the whole nation of Egypt, but I can't handle this. Should I kill them for what they did or forgive them?
A:	Who?
B:	I wasn't talking to you.
Narrator:	Forgiving isn't easy.
B:	You can say that again!
Narrator:	The brothers did come back with the youngest brother, Benjamin.
B:	It's good to see you, Benjamin. Now, all you brothers come and join me for dinner.

A, looking bemused, follows B off stage.

Narrator:	Joseph couldn't resist it. They still had no idea who he was, yet when they sat down to eat, they suddenly realised that they were all sitting in order of their ages—youngest through to oldest. The brothers were gobsmacked. 'How did he do that?' they thought.
B:	*(Comes back in)* This is so hard. I'd love to tell them who I am and forgive them, but I have to test them to see whether they've changed or whether they would still sell their brother as a slave.
Narrator:	I know you, Joseph. You've been up to something. What have you done?
B:	Played a mean trick. I've filled each brother's sack with grain and sent them home.
Narrator:	That's a strange trick.
B:	But I also sneaked a silver cup into Benjamin's sack, and my guards will

	have caught up with them now and searched their sacks. They'll find the silver cup in Benjamin's sack and arrest him. But what will the other brothers do then? Will they try to rescue Benjamin? Or will they abandon him and carry on home without him?
Narrator:	Just like they abandoned you.
B:	Exactly!
A:	*(Rushes in and bows his head)* Please, please, Lord! Take me, arrest me, kill me, but please let Benjamin go! We promised our father, who is now very old, that we would bring Benjamin home. Our father has already lost one son, Joseph, and if he loses Benjamin too it will break his heart. It will kill him. Take me instead, arrest me, kill me, do whatever you like with me, but please, please, please, let Benjamin go home to his father!
B:	Oh, Judah, you have changed so much. You can all go home to your father, and take Benjamin with you.
A:	Oh thank you, my Lord, thank you!
Narrator:	How about Joseph? Would he like to go home too?
A:	What?
B:	*(To A)* It is I!
A:	Pardon?
B:	It's me!
A:	Me who?
B:	Joseph!
A:	Joseph who?
B:	Brother Joseph, who you sold into slavery.
A:	*(Pauses, terrified)* It can't be, you're dea…
B:	*(Interrupts)* Very much alive! Forgiving you all for what you did to me isn't easy, but I can see you have changed. And I forgive you. I want to see Dad, so take some carts and bring him and the rest of the family to Egypt. We can feed you all.
Narrator:	I love a story with a happy ending, and oh boy, Judah had certainly changed. He was even prepared to give his life so that his brother Benjamin could go free—just as Jesus gave his life so that we could be free.

Reproduced with permission from *The Cops & Robbers Holiday Club* by John Hardwick, published by Barnabas for Children 2014: www.barnabasinchurches.org.uk

Quick quiz questions

Quizzes are a wonderful way to recap what the children are learning during their holiday club experience, but they are designed to be fun rather than a measure of the children's knowledge, so do be flexible over some of the answers given. The questions cover general topics as well as specific areas of the programme.

- Question 1 is for the youngest group.
- Question 2 is for the middle group.
- Question 3 is for the older group.
- Question 4 is an extra question if needed.

Day 1: The plot

Which is the odd one out?

1. Police car, police bike, police van or ice cream van? *(Ice cream van)*
2. Police guinea pig, police horse or police dog? *(Police guinea pig)*
3. Police car, ambulance, AA Van or fire engine *(AA van—no blue light)*
4. Clown, police woman, fire fighter or paramedic? *(Clown)*

1. In the puppet sketch, why was Lucy upset? *(Because her little brother has lent out his Beano)*
2. What was she plotting to do? *(Pin him to the washing line, paint his bike pink, steal his teddy bear)*
3. In the Watt family adventure, what are the names of the boy and girl? *(Rick and Wendy)*
4. What terrible crime has been committed? *(Someone has stolen the strawberry cream chocolates)*

1. In the Bible, Eve took what from the tree—a burger, some sweets or a fruit? *(Fruit)*
2. What did Noah build—an ark, a motor bike or an aeroplane? *(Ark)*
3. Daniel was put in a den of kangaroos, monkeys or lions? *(Lions)*
4. Jesus walked on ice cream, water or hot coals? *(Water)*

Day 2: The crime

1. In the puppet sketch, what had Bert done to his little sister's picture? *(Given it to his guinea pig)*
2. What did Lucy say he needed to do? *(Tell the truth and own up)*
3. In the Watt family adventure, what did the robbers leave on Grandma's clean kitchen floor? *(Muddy footprints)*
4. Grandma noticed that they were wearing M&S support tights. Why was this a great clue? *(Mabel had some support tights taken from her washing line)*

1. According to yesterday's Bible verse song, does God have good plans for you or bad plans? *(Good)*
2. How does it make you feel when you know God has good plans for you?

3. Where is the verse found in the Bible? *(Jeremiah 29:11)*
4. Sing the verse. *('I know the plans I have for you,' declares the Lord, 'plans to prosper you and not to harm you, plans to give you hope and a future')*

1. In yesterday's Bible story, what did Joseph's dad give him as a present? *(A colourful coat)*
2. Were Joseph's brothers pleased about the present? *(No)*
3. What was Joseph's first dream and why were his brothers so angry about it? *(Their sheaves of corn bowed down to Joseph's)*
4. What was the second dream and why did it make his brothers and father so cross? *(The sun and moon and eleven stars bowed down before him)*

Day 3: Falsely accused

1. In today's puppet sketch, Bert and Lucy both ended up rather soggy. Why? *(They were cleaning Lucy's dad's car)*
2. Dad was cross. What had happened? *(Water went inside the car)*
3. It appeared that the Watt family had been very naughty. What did Grandma Watt do? *(Stole an iPod from a jogger)*
4. What did Rick do? *(Took a shopper's shopping)*

1. Finish the line or sing Day 2's Bible verse song: 'Always speak the truth and refuse to…'? *(Tell a lie: Proverbs 8:7)*
2. In today's Bible verse, we have to 'hold on tightly'. Sing the verse as a team. *(We can trust God's promises: Hebrews 10:23)*
3. As a team, sing the Bible verse song from Day 1 *('I know the plans I have for you,' declares the Lord, 'plans to prosper you and not to harm you, plans to give you hope and a future')*
4. Choose a Bible verse song to sing.

1. In yesterday's Bible story, Joseph was at home with his dad, but his brothers were at work, looking after which animals? *(Sheep)*
2. Jacob sent Joseph to his brothers. They were not pleased to see him. What did they do to him first of all? *(They grabbed him and threw him down a well)*
3. Then some Ishmaelites, rich men on camels, passed by on the way to Egypt. What did Joseph's brothers do? *(Sold him as a slave)*
4. What did they do to Joseph's coat and who did they have to lie to? *(They ripped his coat and lied to their father Jacob)*

Reproduced with permission from *The Cops & Robbers Holiday Club* by John Hardwick, published by Barnabas for Children 2014: www.barnabasinchurches.org.uk

1. In today's puppet sketch, what had Bert done to his arm and why did it happen? *(He hurt his arm because they played football without any rules)*
2. Oh dear, oh dear, the Watt family were arrested, but how did they have to go to the police station? *(They had to walk because the police cars were all out chasing bank robbers)*
3. They were falsely accused. What actually happened? *(Some people pretended to be the Watt family to get them out of the way)*
4. The detective had a plan in which the Watt family escaped from the police and went on the run. Who would hopefully chase after them? *(The Big Bad Boss's baddies)*

1. As a team, sing a Bible memory verse song.
2. As a team, sing a different Bible memory verse song.
3. As a team, sing another Bible memory verse song.
4. As a team, sing today's song.

1. In yesterday's Bible story, Joseph was sold by his brother for 20 pieces of silver. What country did they take him to? *(Egypt)*
2. What was the name of the man who bought him in Egypt? (Clue: think of a pot) *(Potiphar)*
3. God was with Joseph and he became head of the household, but then what happened? *(Potiphar's wife took a fancy to him and falsely accused him)*
4. What happened to Joseph? *(He was flung into jail)*

2. Joseph then went to tell the king what his dream meant. What did the seven fat cows mean and what did the seven thin cows that ate the fat cows mean? *(Seven years of good harvest, followed by seven years of famine)*
3. What did Joseph suggest they do? *(Build big cities to store food)*
4. Who became the second most powerful man in all of Egypt? *(Joseph)*

1. In today's puppet sketch, Lucy struggled to forgive her friends. What had they forgotten to do? *(Take her to the circus)*
2. In today's Watt family adventure, who tracked down the Big Bad Boss's hideout? *(The Watt family)*
3. The Big Bad Boss's gang managed to capture the Watt family, but the Big Bad Boss got a phone call that upset him. Why? *(His house had been burgled)*
4. The Watt family were upset too. Why? *(Because no one deserves to be burgled like that)*

1. As a team, sing a Bible memory verse song.
2. As a team, sing a different Bible memory verse song.
3. As a team, sing another Bible memory verse song.
4. And another!

1. In yesterday's Bible story, the king's cupbearer and baker had dreams. Who told them what the dreams meant? *(Joseph, with God's help)*

Reproduced with permission from *The Cops & Robbers Holiday Club* by John Hardwick, published by Barnabas for Children 2014: www.barnabasinchurches.org.uk

Cops & Robbers
fun sheets

Day 1: The plot

Don't be jealous!

Check out the Bible story in Genesis 37:1-11.

Help Joe find his new coat!

Spot ten differences below.

Find the good and bad words in the word search below: James 3 16 17 jealous, selfish, trouble, cruel, wisdom, pure, friendly, gentle, sensible, kind, helpful, genuine, sincere

c	3	e	m	o	d	s	i	w
d	r	l	6	j	a	m	e	s
e	n	u	g	e	n	t	l	e
n	c	i	e	a	l	7	f	n
i	j	o	k	l	p	s	r	s
u	e	n	p	o	e	e	i	i
n	t	r	o	u	b	l	e	b
e	r	o	u	s	s	f	n	l
g	b	b	e	p	r	I	d	e
e	r	e	c	n	i	s	l	t
l	u	f	p	l	e	h	y	o

'I know the plans I have for you,' declares the Lord.

(JEREMIAH 29:11, NIV)

www.johnhardwick.org.uk

Day 2: The crime

Speak the truth!

Check out the Bible story in Genesis 37:12-36.

Help Joe out of the well.

Spot ten differences below and colour the picture.

Bible memory verse:

I / a _ w _ _ _ / _ _ e _ _ / _ _ _ / _ r t _ / a _ _ /

r _ f _ _ _ / _ _ / _ _ _ _ / a / l _ _ / P _ _ v _ _ b _ / _ V _ /

Colour Joe's coat before it gets ruined!

Find the words in the word search below:
dreamer, sheaves, corn, stars, sun, eleven, brothers, Joseph, coat, well, sold, 20, shekels, slave, Egypt, speak, truth, don't, lie

s	t	r	e	m	a	e	r	d
p	b	J	o	s	e	p	h	n
e	t	r	w	e	l	l	u	k
a	o	s	o	l	d	s	c	c
k	t	r	u	t	h	n	o	t
e	n'	n	m	e	h	a	r	l
v	o	e	a	p	t	e	n	i
a	d	v	r	2	0	y	r	e
l	e	e	v	s	r	a	t	s
s	a	l	E	g	y	p	t	u
s	l	e	k	e	h	s	u	p

Day 3: Falsely accused

Hold on tightly!

Check out the Bible story in Genesis 39.

Help Joe escape from Potiphar's wife!

Spot nine differences below.

Come back, good-looking!

No way!

Find the words in the word search below:
Joe, good, servant, resist, temptation,
Potiphar, house, wife, lied, run, away,
robe, falsely, accused, go, to, jail

Say NO to temptation!

Bible memory verse: Hebrews 10:23–25

We must hold on t _ _ _ _ ly to the h_ _ _ that
we say is ours. After all, w_ can t _ _ _ _ the
one who m_ _ _ the ag _ _ _ _ _ _ _ with us.

g	p	t	n	a	v	r	e	s
t	o	i	e	g	o	e	u	u
e	e	o	t	m	P	r	b	n
m	j	d	d	t	o	l	e	f
p	a	e	t	b	t	f	n	a
t	i	s	e	a	i	d	e	l
a	c	u	J	w	p	e	s	s
t	o	c	o	a	h	i	u	e
i	a	c	e	y	a	l	o	l
o	j	a	i	l	r	x	h	y
n	r	e	s	i	s	t	y	z

www.johnhardwick.org.uk

Day 4: *Go to jail*

Jail-break to freedom!

Check out the Bible story in Genesis 40.

Help Joe find his way out of jail!

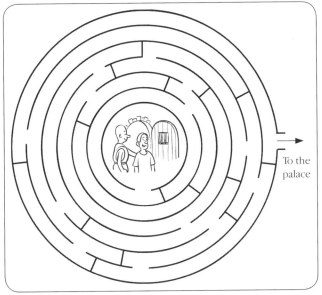

To the palace

How many words can you make out of FREEDOM?

Spot ten differences below.

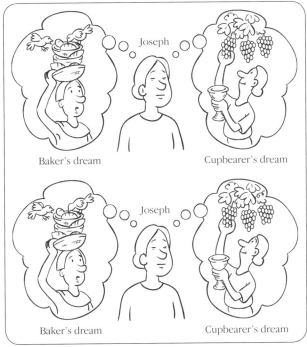

Baker's dream   Joseph   Cupbearer's dream

Baker's dream   Joseph   Cupbearer's dream

F = Forgiven: God has forgiven me.
R = Rescued: Jesus has saved me.
E = Everlasting: God is with me for ever.
E = Enjoy: God wants me to enjoy my life with him.

Fill in the missing letters in the gaps to find today's Bible memory verses.

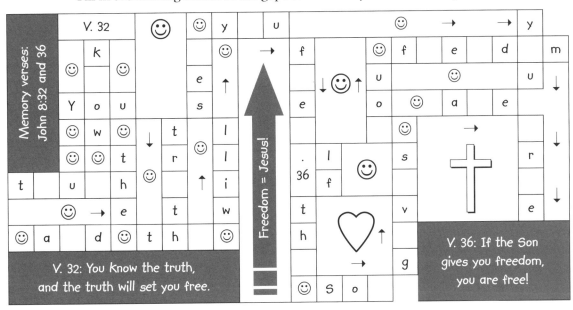

Memory verses: John 8:32 and 36

Freedom = Jesus!

V. 32: You know the truth, and the truth will set you free.

V. 36: If the Son gives you freedom, you are free!

Day 5: Forgiveness isn't easy

Hard choices

Check out the Bible story in Genesis 42–45.

Help Joe's brothers find their way home and colour the picture.

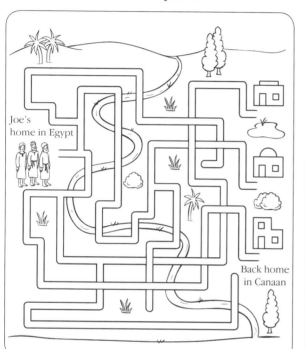

Spot ten differences below.

Joseph had eleven brothers. Write down the names of people in your family. Are we always kind to one another and do we forgive each other?

Find the words in the word search below: 7, years, of, famine, Joe's, brothers, buy, food, spies, steal, silver, cup, sack, weep, Benjamin, forgiven, together, again

b	r	o	t	h	e	r	s	w
u	f	a	m	i	n	e	s	e
y	n	c	u	b	f	e	a	e
e	e	a	7	n	i	n	c	p
a	v	n	i	þ	i	n	k	u
r	i	a	s	i	l	v	e	r
s	g	f	d	s	i	c	k	l
a	r	o	's	k	t	j	u	c
t	o	g	e	t	h	e	r	p
f	f	j	o	w	k	c	a	r
b	e	n	j	a	m	i	n	l

Be kind and compassionate to one another, forgiving each other, just as in Christ God forgave you.

(EPHESIANS 4:32, NIV)

Reproduced with permission from *The Cops & Robbers Holiday Club* by John Hardwick, published by Barnabas for Children 2014: www.barnabasinchurches.org.uk

78

www.johnhardwick.org.uk

Appendices

Cops & Robbers policeman's cap

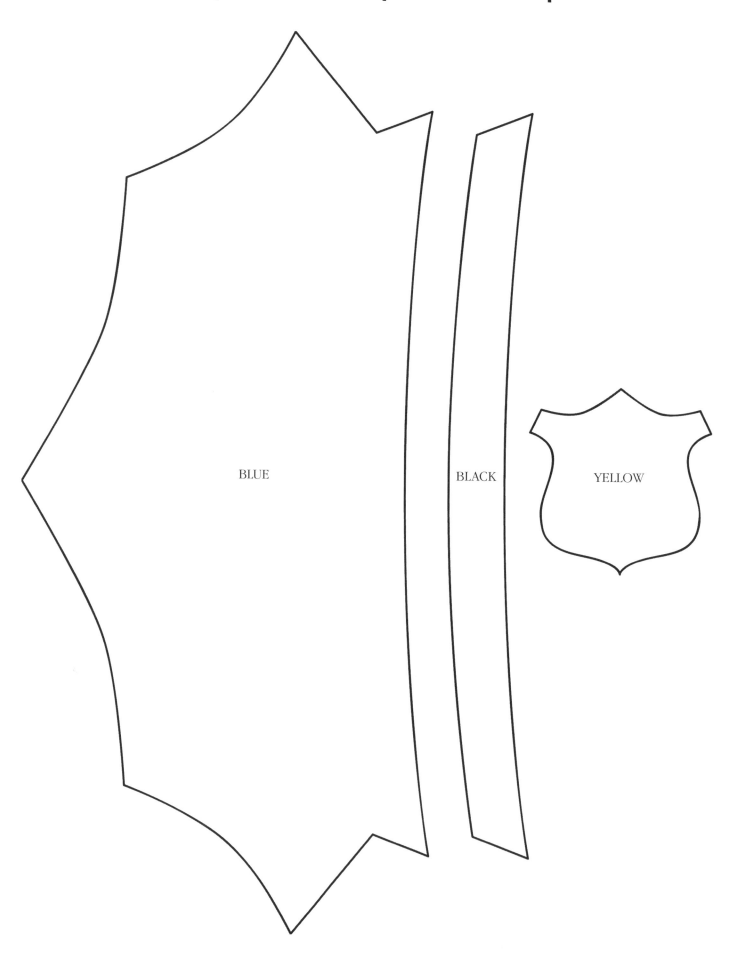

BLUE

BLACK

YELLOW

Cops & Robbers finger puppets

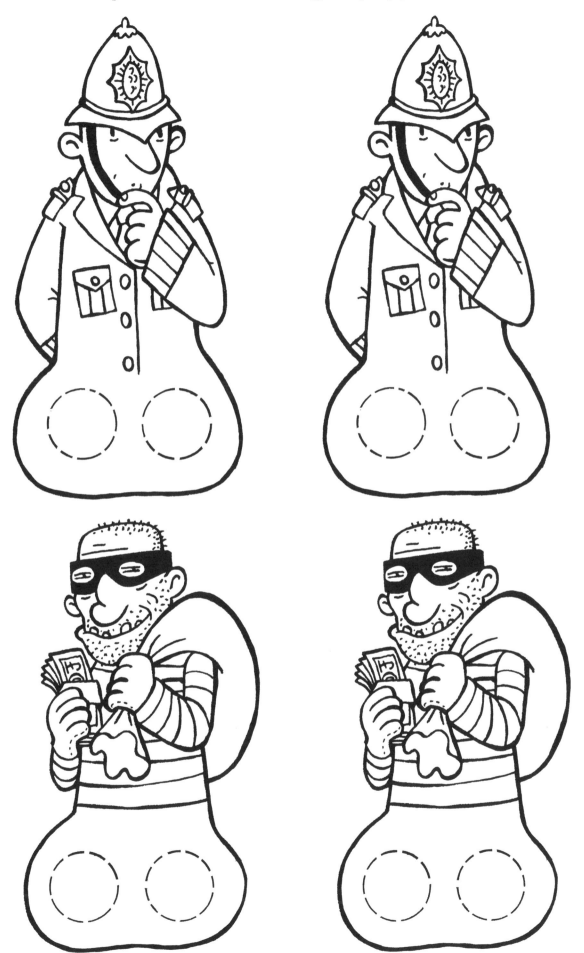

Cops & Robbers pop-up puppet

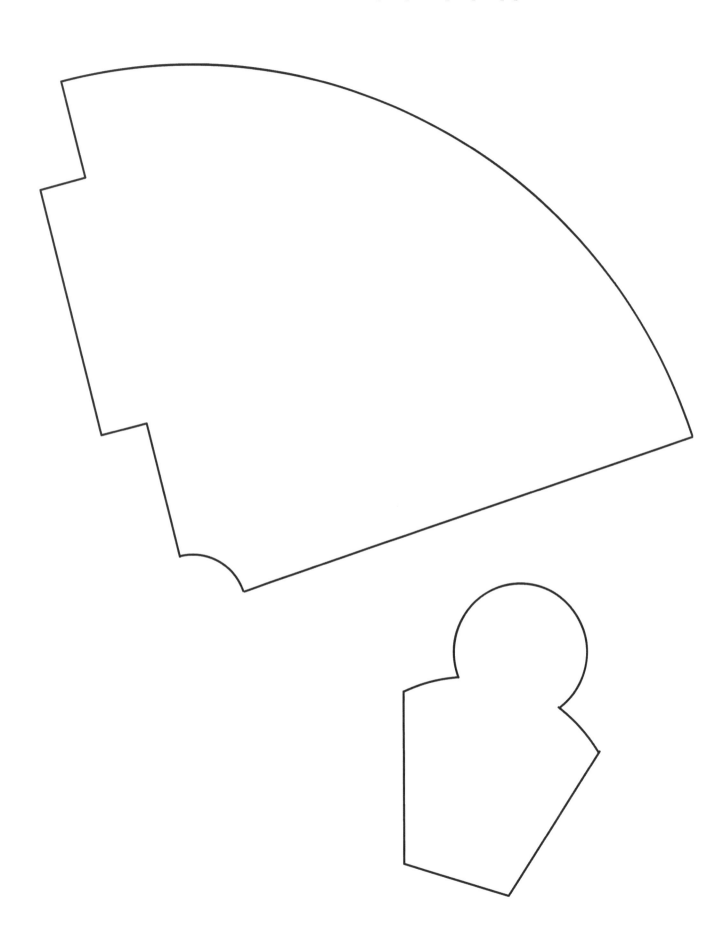

Cops & Robbers mask

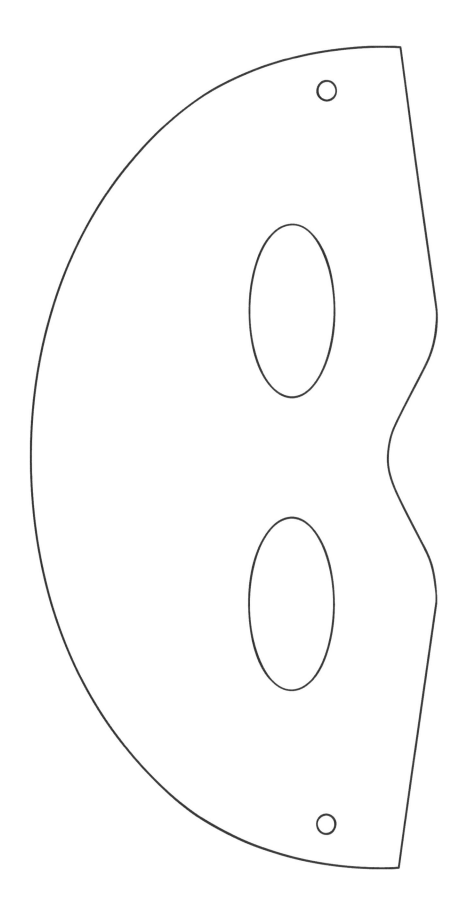

Cops & Robbers badges

Use the templates below to make badges for the children. Photocopy on to thin card and attach a safety pin to the back with a strip of masking tape. The children can colour in their own badges and write their names in the space. Younger children might need team leaders to help them write their names.

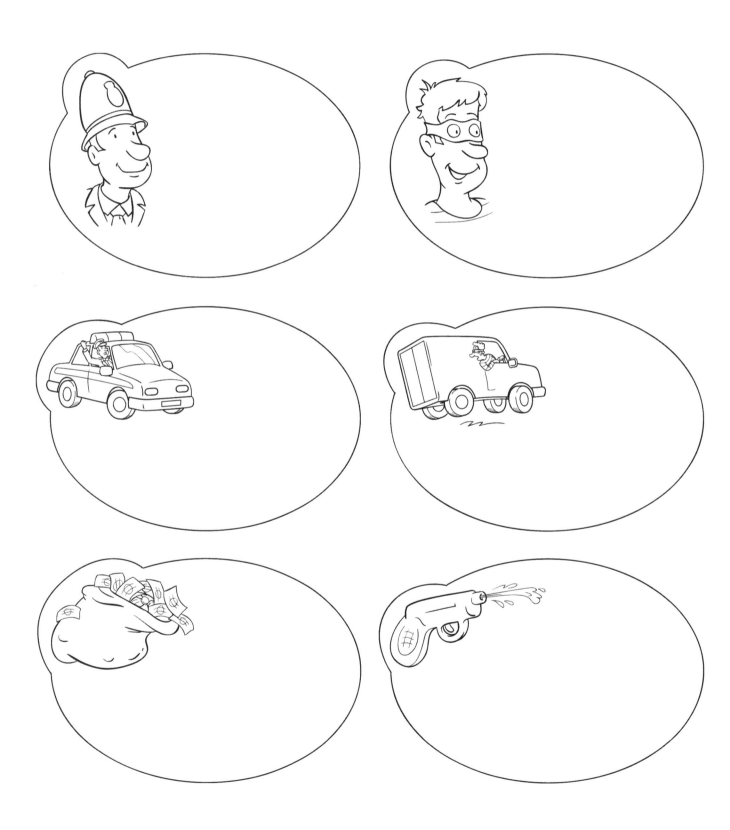

Cops & Robbers invitation cards

Photocopy the templates below to make invitation cards for your Cops & Robbers holiday club. The children can colour them in and give them out to their friends and classmates.

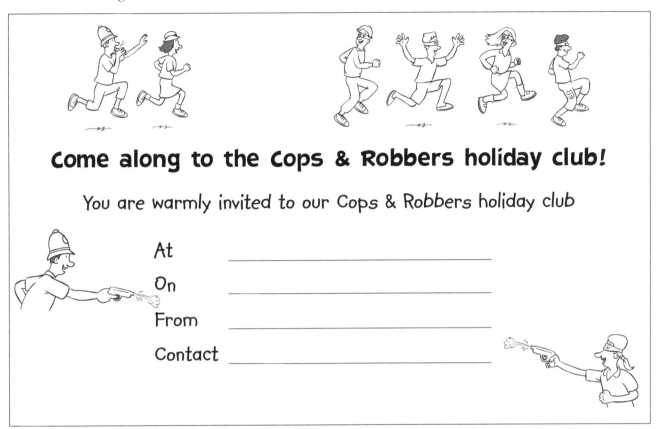

Come along to the Cops & Robbers holiday club!

You are warmly invited to our Cops & Robbers holiday club

At _____

On _____

From _____

Contact _____

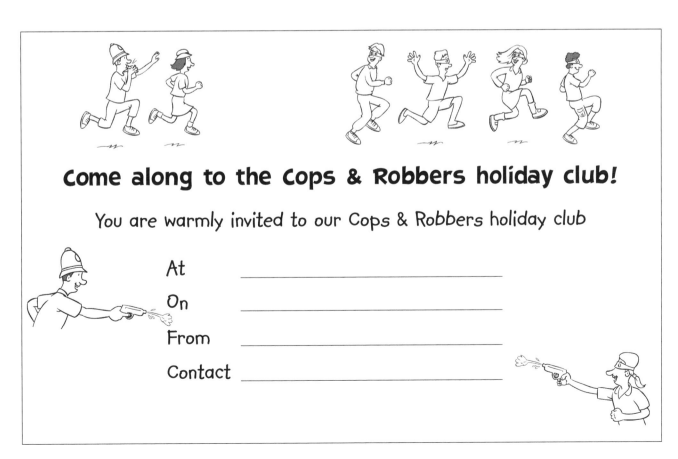

Come along to the Cops & Robbers holiday club!

You are warmly invited to our Cops & Robbers holiday club

At _____

On _____

From _____

Contact _____

Cops & Robbers registration form

Cops & Robbers

Name _____

Address _____

_____

Date of birth _____   Landline _____

Mobile _____   Email _____

Contact in case of emergency _____

Second contact in case of emergency _____

Special needs, including allergies and medication _____

_____

School attended _____

Church attended _____

I hereby give permission for _____ (name of child)

to take part in activities at _____ (name of venue)

and my consent for medical treatment or first aid arising out of illness or accident.

Signed (Parent/guardian) _____

Date _____

Cops & Robbers presentation poster

Use this poster to invite parents, carers, relatives and friends to a Cops & Robbers event to find out what the children have been doing during the club time.

Please come along to our
Cops & Robbers
presentation

At _____

On _____

Time _____

Reproduced with permission from *The Cops & Robbers Holiday Club* by John Hardwick, published by Barnabas for Children 2014: www.barnabasinchurches.org.uk

Fun sheet answers

Fun sheet One

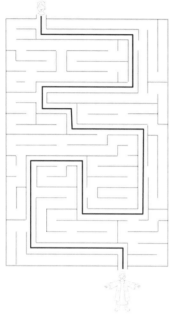

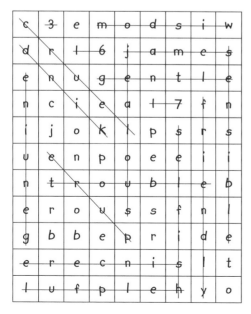

Fun sheet Two

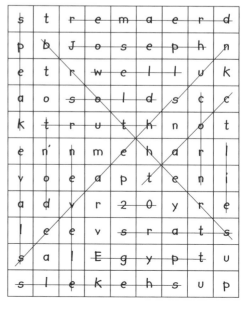

Fun sheet answers

Fun sheet Three

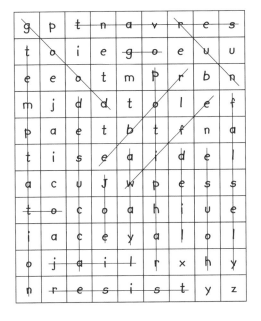

Fun sheet Four

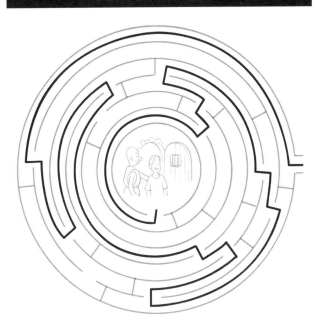

Fun sheet answers

Fun sheet Five

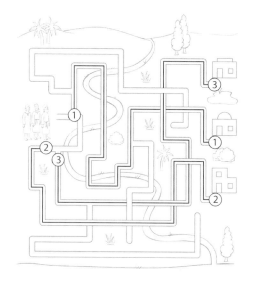

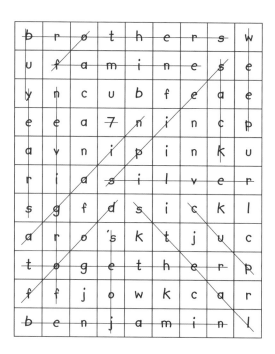

John Hardwick works under the banner of Counties and GenR8 to present the Christian message in an exciting way, which will appeal to people of all ages. Equally well received in schools, churches and at outreach events, John works with children and families of all ages and backgrounds. He juggles and sings and tells stories for the King of kings. John leads Creative Communications training events for those involved in children's ministry and all-age services, where his workshops include key areas such as storytelling and presenting the Bible through music. John is a recording artist, recording Bible stories, songs and sketches, and produces DVDs of his work. He also organises sessions for worship leaders, family and all-age services and holiday clubs. John is a familiar face at Spring Harvest, Easter People and other Christian events, where he leads family and children's sessions. John is a member of the Barnabas Children's Ministry team and author of a wealth of holiday club resources, including *Champions!*, *Junior Heroes!*, *Starship Discovery*, *Razzamatazz Robots*, *Sports Academy* and *Adventure Cruise*, all published by Barnabas for Children.

Further resources

Printed resources

- Luke's Gospel (Easy English) (Bible Society)
- Luke's Gospel (ESV) (Bible Society)
- John's Gospel (GNB) (Bible Society)
- New Testament (ESV) (Bible Society)
- New Testament and Psalms (NSRV) (Bible Society)
- New Testament and Psalms (CEV) (Bible Society)
- The Barnabas Children's Bible (Barnabas for Children)
- and give-away NIV Gospel/New Testament (Hodder/Biblica)
- Evangelistic booklet for church events (Good Book Company)
- Gospel in magazine format for kids (UCB)
- Special Word for Today (UCB)
- One-off tracts (UCB)
- 'How to' book/DVD: Just do it (Salvation Army)
- Pin badges, stickers and so on (CPO)

Music

The *Cops & Robbers* master CD is available from John's website: www.johnhardwick.org.uk. This CD includes the theme song, all the Bible verse songs and the Joseph Bible stories.

Not only is this a great resource to use during the holiday club, but you can make copies of the master CD to give to the children—a great memento, which children will play long after the club ends.

There are scripted narrations for the Joseph Bible stories on pages 58–67, but if you are struggling to find a team or storyteller who is able to bring the Bible stories to life, then the recording on John's CD could be a great resource. You can find free downloadable pictures of the whole of the Joseph story at www.freebibleimages.org.

A DVD and CD package is also available direct from www.johnhardwick.org.uk.

Other resources include:

- *Action Packed Praise* 1 and 2 (DVD and CD of John's songs)
- *Christmas Rock*: a Christmas rock 'n' roll-style musical based on the nativity story, ideal as a Christmas special follow-up for holiday clubs or Messy Church. The musical can be performed by churches or KS2/P4–7 children in schools. The material also works well as a puppet show musical. Available from www.johnhardwick.org.uk.
- YouTube: You can also find some of John Hardwick's songs on YouTube.
- Social networking: Join a group on Facebook. Search for Holiday Clubs and VBS by John Hardwick. See what other people have done with the themes and share ideas. You can also see crafts, games and photographs, and watch video clips on the site.

Stay legal!

Please remember to tick any songs used during your holiday club or in your weekly church services on your Christian Copyright Licence (CCL) list.

Training events

Schools work

John is a member of the Barnabas Children's Ministry team and offers full-day RE presentations bringing the Bible to life through the creative arts, including music, creative storytelling, puppetry and circus skills. A typical day with John might include:

- A 20-minute assembly with the theme 'Working together and valuing one another'. The assembly includes a juggling talk, song and Bible story told in a dramatic way and is suitable for Collective Worship across Key Stages 1 and 2 / P1–7.
- A 40- to 50-minute assembly with the theme 'Creation appreciation', leading into 'Our uniqueness' and how we need to show respect and compassion for others. This is John's most popular theme and could be shortened for younger children. The presentation includes Bible stories told in a dramatic way, a creative poem, a puppet sketch, music and songs, a juggling story with a diabolo, questions and plenty of participation. Ideally, the presentation needs to take place in the school hall or similar space. The material is designed to meet the needs of different year groups across Key Stages 1 and 2 / P1–7 and could be repeated with each year group as required.
- A 30-minute class or year group presentation exploring the value of books and the Bible. This includes a Bible story told in a dramatic way, a puppet sketch, song, juggling, unicycling and other circus skills. Ideally, the presentation needs to take place in the school hall or similar space. The material is designed to meet the needs of different year groups across Key Stages 1 and 2 / P1–7 and will be repeated with each year group as required.
- A 'circus skills' workshop suitable for Years 5 and 6. The workshop offers the opportunity for pupils to try their hand at skills such as juggling, plate-spinning, stunt sticks and diabolos. Maximum number per group: 30 children.

To book John for a Barnabas RE day, or for further details, contact:

BRF, 15 The Chambers, Vineyard, Abingdon, OX14 3FE
Telephone: 01865 319700; Fax: 01865 319701
E-mail: enquiries@brf.org.uk
Website: www.barnabasinchurches.org.uk

Training events

John Hardwick also offers a range of training events, including the following.

- Creative communication training days or sessions: Training days provide a feast of ideas, with a particular focus on storytelling, puppets and music. Ideal for anyone involved in leading services and events where children are present.
- Cool and Crazy praise parties: Praise parties are high-energy, fast-moving sessions for families with primary-aged children. John juggles and sings and tells stories for the King.
- Songs for every occasion: New songs sessions provide a chance to see John's infectious songs in action.
- All-age services: All-age services provide plenty of variety with a message for everyone.
- Holiday clubs: John offers a fun-packed holiday club package including stage-based presentations, songs, Bible narrations and puppetry.

For further information about any of the above products or events, please contact:

John Hardwick
2 Lucketts Close
Histon
Cambridge
CB24 9HG

E-mail: johnhardwick36@hotmail.com
Website: www.johnhardwick.org.uk

Sample session from *Hanging Out with Jesus* (Barnabas for Children, 2013), ISBN 9781841017907, £8.99. This resource offers six interactive Bible studies for 9–14s.

Session 1

Sitting with Jesus

It has been said that for their first two years, children are encouraged to walk and talk, and for the next 16, they are told to sit down and shut up! Sitting still and remaining quiet does not always come naturally to young people, particularly when it's enforced. One of the discoveries of growing older, however, is that being still and quiet makes us receptive, which is why we must sometimes choose to do it. It is important for all sorts of activities—getting to know friends, listening in lessons and even watching TV.

The story of Mary and Martha in the Bible is about a choice between being busy and being still, on an occasion where stillness was more important. It is an influential story for Christians, who have believed for centuries that it's important once in a while just to stop, because that's the best chance we have of clearing our minds and noticing things that God might want us to think about.

Starting

Make sure that the area you're using is comfortable and relaxed. If possible, have soft chairs or beanbags available to sit on, arranged in a circle.

Once everyone has arrived (and had a drink and a biscuit), ask the young people about sitting still. Can they think of places where they like sitting still and others where they hate it? When they're at home or at school, who sits around a lot and who rushes about? Do they know anyone who never stops rushing around?

Now try an experiment. Ask your group to be still and silent for one minute. See if they can manage it. Then ask the group how they found the exercise. Was it easy? What distractions were there? What was going through their minds? Did their bodies want to stay still? What's the point of a game like this?

Using the prompt sheet

Hand round the prompt sheets (see page 19) and ask the members of the group to spend a bit of time completing them. Then compare their answers.

Group members may suggest 'church' as a place where you have to be quiet. It may be worth asking the whole group about this. Does everyone agree? Why are people quiet in church? Are all churches like this?

Don't be afraid to go off at tangents. If someone has a funny story about sitting at someone's feet, let everyone hear it: it's all part of the fun of a group conversation.

The question in the middle of the prompt sheet, about whether it is better to sit down or be busy in the kitchen, is a deliberately odd question, intended to arouse curiosity. It is, of course, a lead in to the Bible study.

Martha and Mary

Hand round some Bibles and ask everyone to look up Luke 10:38–42. Read the passage and then ask the group some questions.

- Look at verse 39. What sort of thing do you think Jesus might have been talking about that Mary found so interesting?
- Martha was doing all the work by herself (v. 40). Do you feel sorry for her?
- Jesus says that 'only one thing is necessary' and that 'Mary has chosen what is best' (v. 42). What exactly was the thing that Mary chose?
- Do you think this story means that when someone at home asks you to help with the housework, you have a biblical reason to refuse?

Time out for God

Explain that, because of stories like this, Christians often choose to be still and quiet. This has a purpose: they want to focus on God and on what he has to say to us.

Just as Mary chose to sit and listen to Jesus, the group now has a chance to try out the same thing. Spending time in silence may feel a bit odd at first (especially if they found one minute hard at the start of the session), but it won't be for very long and they may learn to enjoy the calm of this special time that has been set aside.

Show the group around the space that you have arranged for the quiet time, and point out any books, CD or mp3 players, art materials, writing materials or other resources that will be available. If people in the group have mobile phones, it is a good idea to collect them in a bag that you will keep in a safe place. Handing over mobiles is a sign that you are committed to avoiding distractions.

Before the quiet time begins, go round the group and ask everyone to say which activity they have chosen to do. Encourage anyone who hasn't decided at least to say where they are going to start. Mention that you will let everyone know when the time is up.

Then leave them to it. Position yourself somewhere inconspicuous but where you can still see what is going on. Quietly intervene if anyone is being distracting or disruptive: ask how they are finding the exercise, and ask them to remain quiet for the sake of the others in the group. Ten or 15 minutes is probably long enough for this first go at 'time out'.

Afterwards

Ask the members of the group to sit together again and briefly ask how they found the time they have just spent. Did they enjoy it?

Consider for a moment the following groups of people who regularly set aside time to be still before God. What do you think of each of these? Do you think you could manage what they do? If you have access to the internet, you could show web pages and video clips for each of the groups.

- The Taizé Community: people from across the world, living and working together, welcoming over 100,000 young people every year to live simply and spend time in prayer and worship.
- 24/7 Prayer: an organisation that encourages people to pray at regular points in the day (whatever they are doing) and has someone, somewhere in the world, praying at this and every moment.
- Monks and nuns: people who follow special rules for living, including vows that they will not do certain things (like getting married) and will do other things (like attending services every day).

Finishing

To finish the session, pass round a plate of small chocolates, sweets or biscuits. Before each member of the group can take their sweet, they must name one thing that has particularly made them think.

Alternatively, you might like to finish on a light-hearted note by playing some group games. Consider the following loud and quiet games:

Shouting game

Group members pair up and then stand on opposite sides of the room. One person is given a Bible verse; the other has a pen and paper. The person with the verse must shout it across the room for the other person to write down (over the noise of all the other pairs doing the same thing).

Bunch of keys game

One person is blindfolded and sits on a chair or stool. A big bunch of keys is placed under the chair. In complete silence, another member of the group is nominated to creep forward and try to steal the noisy keys from under the chair without the blindfolded person detecting them and touching them.

Sleeping lions

Everyone in the group lies completely still on the floor, apart from one or two 'rangers' who roam around trying to get the 'lions' to move or make a noise. The rangers cannot touch the lions but can wave their arms, tell jokes, sing badly and so on.

Guess a minute

An adult with a watch says 'Go' and times one minute. Everyone in the group has to bury their head in their arms and guess when a minute has elapsed, after which they stand up and call out 'That's a minute!' The person who gets closest wins. (Make sure people take their watches off for this game!)

Sitting with Jesus

Are you ever lazy? Tick the box.

yes ☐ no ☐

Occasional itch

0 ← Asleep ⊙ Ants in pants → 10

How fidgety are you feeling right now?

Add an arrow to the Fidget-o-meter.

This person is sitting down

Which is better?

This person is very busy in the Kitchen

3 places where you have to be busy
1. ....
2. ....
3. ....

3 places where you have to be quiet
1. ....
2. ....
3. ....

Have you sat at anyone's feet recently... and did they smell all right?

Enjoyed
this book?

Write a review—we'd love to hear what you think. Email: reviews@brf.org.uk

Keep up to date—receive details of our new books as they happen.
Sign up for email news and select your interest groups at:
www.brfonline.org.uk/findoutmore/

Follow us on Twitter @brfonline

By post—to receive new title information by post (UK only), complete the form below and post to: BRF Mailing Lists, 15 The Chambers, Vineyard, Abingdon, Oxfordshire, OX14 3FE

Your Details
Name _____
Address_____
_____
Town/City _____ Post Code _____
Email _____

Your Interest Groups (*Please tick as appropriate)

- ☐ Advent/Lent
- ☐ Bible Reading & Study
- ☐ Children's Books
- ☐ Discipleship
- ☐ Leadership
- ☐ Messy Church
- ☐ Pastoral
- ☐ Prayer & Spirituality
- ☐ Resources for Children's Church
- ☐ Resources for Schools

Support your local bookshop
Ask about their new title information schemes.